D0093088

The joy of missing out belongs to:

- -

JOMO

Celebrate the Joy of Missing Out!

JESSICA MISENER

ADAMS MEDIA

NEW YORK   LONDON   TORONTO   SYDNEY   NEW DELHI

Adams Media
An Imprint of Simon & Schuster, Inc.
57 Littlefield Street
Avon, Massachusetts 02322

Copyright © 2019 by Simon & Schuster, Inc.

All rights reserved, including the right to reproduce this book or portions thereof in any form whatsoever. For information address Adams Media Subsidiary Rights Department, 1230 Avenue of the Americas, New York, NY 10020.

First Adams Media hardcover edition November 2019

ADAMS MEDIA and colophon are trademarks of Simon & Schuster.

For information about special discounts for bulk purchases, please contact Simon & Schuster Special Sales at 1-866-506-1949 or business@simonandschuster .com.

The Simon & Schuster Speakers Bureau can bring authors to your live event. For more information or to book an event contact the Simon & Schuster Speakers Bureau at 1-866-248-3049 or visit our website at www.simonspeakers.com.

Interior design by Colleen Cunningham

Manufactured in the United States of America

10 9 8 7 6 5 4 3 2 1

Library of Congress Cataloging-in-Publication Data has been applied for.

ISBN 978-1-5072-1142-7
ISBN 978-1-5072-1143-4 (ebook)

Many of the designations used by manufacturers and sellers to distinguish their products are claimed as trademarks. Where those designations appear in this book and Simon & Schuster, Inc., was aware of a trademark claim, the designations have been printed with initial capital letters.

For Mike, my favorite person to miss out with.

Introduction

Have you ever felt that little thrill when a friend cancels your plans to go out that night? Maybe you've seen a crowded party going down on *Instagram* and felt even happier with your decision to set up shop on the couch. There's actually a name for that feeling! It's called JOMO, or the joy of missing out.

JOMO is about taking time for yourself—time you may need to recharge in your own space, or simply want in order to enjoy your favorite at-home activities. It means putting your happiness first and ignoring the pressure to go out to that club/to that dinner/to whatever else you felt you *should* do. Because skipping a night on the town doesn't mean you're missing out on life—you're just missing out on someone else's idea of what your life should look like.

The Joy of Missing Out is full of fun, unique ways to celebrate this time spent at home—whether alone, with a partner or friend, or as a group. It's time to kick guilt to the curb and celebrate staying in—and this book is here to help. You'll find more than 350 activities ranging from the simple to the more involved, including:

- Concocting a crazy new ice cream flavor
- Learning how to moonwalk
- Hosting a Crock-Pot cook-off
- Celebrating a hashtag-free Throwback Thursday

- Having a paper airplane battle
- Relaxing with a homemade spa treatment
- Writing to a pen pal

Whether slipping into your coziest pajamas for a movie marathon or throwing a karaoke night for your closest friends, you've made the right choice—so stop worrying. Instead, let your inner homebody run free and relish in the joy of missing out!

Celebrate a Hashtag-Free Throwback Thursday

Put your smartphone away and dig up your old photo albums or prints (remember those?) from when you were younger. Even if you're glad the days of bad haircuts are (hopefully) done, you'll enjoy waxing nostalgic about the past. Not ready to revisit cringe-worthy memories? You can pore through photos of your parents or grandparents from when they were your age instead.

To make it a group affair, you can throw a #ThrowbackThursday party where guests dress in favorite retro looks and bring along some of their most embarrassing or hilarious photos from a time before everyone had cameras in their pockets.

Make Homemade Ice Cream

What's even better than a carton of store-bought ice cream or a cone from your local shop? Churning up a big batch right in the comfort of your own kitchen! Ice cream makers are simple to use and inexpensive to buy online or at your local big-box retailer. You can make the custard base ahead of time using whatever flavors you'd like—vanilla, cookie dough, even lavender honey—then simply pour it into the machine, hit the start button, and come back minutes later to a delectable homemade dessert. And with a home-made mixer, you're not limited to store-bought flavors: You can mix up any crazy combinations you think of, from chocolate and sage to a goat cheese and blackberry swirl.

Spark Your Inner Baker (or Sweet Tooth) with *The Great British Baking Show*

What is it about this show that's so calming? Let the dulcet accents, drool-worthy creations, and friendly contestants lull you into a state of total serenity (and some extreme sugar cravings). Who knows, you may feel inspired to whip up a batch of Chelsea buns, savory tartlets, or a rough puff pastry in your own kitchen.

Explore Virtual Reality

Buy (or borrow) a VR headset and navigate the crazy technology of virtual reality—in the comfort of your own home! With this immersive headset strapped on, you'll quickly lose sight of any stress you may have been feeling. Make the most of your time-out from normal life by touring a jungle, biking through Yellowstone National Park, or just going full zen on a virtual beach.

Play Your Favorite Childhood Card Game

Were you a junior Uno champion? A connoisseur of Crazy Eights? An expert angler in Go Fish? Relive your glory days with a simple deck of cards, a few close friends, and some competitive spirit. See if you still have your mojo after all these years.

Collect a Compliments File

When challenging situations or negative thoughts make you doubt yourself, you need some concrete evidence of how awesome you really are! Take advantage of this reflective time alone by creating a "brag book" of all those little reminders that you're crushing it in life. You can refer to your collection of accolades when you're feeling less than 100 percent confident (and let's face it, no one feels completely confident all of the time). Here are some things you can include in your compliments file:

- An email from your boss about how you mastered that presentation
- Any work samples you're proud of, like reports or newsletters or data analyses
- A list of compliments you've gotten in your lifetime that have stuck with you
- Scholarships or awards you've received
- A really killer performance evaluation you got at work
- A copy of your college transcript from when you rocked that difficult math course
- Positive feedback from friends or family members on a hobby or talent
- Thank-you notes and nice letters

Keep adding to your file whenever you receive praise, and store it in a space you have easy access to so you can revisit it whenever you need a little self-esteem boost.

Go Camping in Your Backyard

Who says you need to hike way out into the wilderness to really enjoy the great outdoors? Grab a tent, some sleeping bags and blankets, and your favorite snacks, and spend a night in nature (kind of). Bonus: When you camp in your own yard, a *real* bathroom is only a few yards away!

Watch *The Princess Bride*

It's inconceivable that you haven't seen this 1987 classic adventure film, so give it a rewatch (or a first watch if you *have* managed to get this far in life without seeing it) when you want a laid-back night in. Not only is the story fun, but countless lines have become classic pop culture quotes that you'll be able to trade back and forth with your friends.

Change Your Phone Background

Since you can't avoid your phone forever, turn checking your notifications into an opportunity for joy with a photo background that makes you smile. Some ideas: your significant other, a pet, your childhood home, or a pretty nature scene.

Plan Your Fantasy Music Festival

No doubt you've seen the highlights of festival life all over social media, from mouthwatering fair food like fried chicken doughnuts, to trendy fringed outfits and selfies with A-list celebrities. But all those picture-perfect moments require a lot of time, money, and travel—not to mention wading through a huge sea of people just to catch a glimpse of your favorite act. If your style is more *Couch-ella* than Coachella, you can bring dozens of your favorite artists together in one cozy place: your own living room.

Crack open your laptop and design a lineup for the festival of your dreams. You control the set lists! Is it Metallica playing alongside Ariana Grande and Kacey Musgraves? Drake rubbing elbows with Beyoncé? Or maybe Fleetwood Mac performing a duet with Lorde? Have fun creating a music event that's uniquely you. If you're feeling extra artistic, you can also design a poster for your custom festival, or build a *YouTube* playlist of your favorite artists' live performances to feel like you're really there.

Design Your Dream Backyard

Bistro lights, a koi pond, fire pits, and comfy hammocks: A great backyard can bring a little bit of zen and the perfect environment for recharging at your own home. Surf *Pinterest* or interior design blogs and build a mockup of your perfect backyard setup. Maybe you dream of having your own private hot tub, or would love to replace that old tool shed with a fully equipped gaming den. Even if renovating your yard is financially out of reach for now, it never hurts to have a dream. You can still relax by *imagining* yourself chilling in that Adirondack chair!

Carve a Pumpkin

Who said it has to be October to get in a spooky spirit? Make the most of your pre-autumn time by practicing your ideal jack-o'-lantern face so you'll be Halloween ready. Plus, you can use the pumpkin innards and seeds in your cooking! (If pumpkins aren't in season, you can carve a watermelon or butternut squash.) To get started, spread out some newspaper so you don't end up with a kitchen covered in pumpkin. Cut off the "lid" of the pumpkin and scoop out the seeds. Next, draw your face or scene on the outside of the pumpkin, then carefully carve it out with a sharp knife. Light a tealight or votive inside your creation. Boo!

Revamp Your Bubble Bath

Infuse your self-care soak with a fun whirlwind of scent and color via a bath bomb (or three). Stock up on these fizzy treats from stores like Lush and Bath & Body Works. You can find bombs of all shapes, sizes, colors, and even consistencies that will fill your bath with rose petals, lavender oil, aloe gel, or a sparkly explosion of glitter.

Read *The Great Gatsby*

Get jazzed on the glamour of the roaring twenties in F. Scott Fitzgerald's classic 1925 novel featuring the romantic Jay, enchanting Daisy, and other glitzy characters in pursuit of the American dream. When you're done, check out a film version of Fitzgerald's book and see how it holds up.

Make Cookie Dough

Baking takes time, which you don't always have the patience for when you need your cookie fix now. Whip up a batch of egg-free cookie dough and enjoy your sweet treat with a spoon.

Write *Yelp* Reviews for Your Favorite Spots

People often head to *Yelp* to air their grievances about a restaurant's service or complain about a lukewarm cup of coffee. How about putting out some positive vibes instead? Find the *Yelp* page for your favorite café, dinner spot, dry cleaner, or boutique and write a sincere review about why this place excels at what they do. The owners will be grateful for your thoughtful praise, you'll tip off future customers, and you'll reap good karma next time you're there.

Challenge Yourself to a HIIT Workout

HIIT, or high-intensity interval training, is a killer workout that uses quick interval exercises to pump up your heart rate and pack in both cardio and strength training. Think burpees, jumping jacks, squats, and lunges. By alternating between doing these moves at your fastest possible pace and at a very slow pace, you gain the maximum benefits. Since all you need is your body, pick a routine from countless options online and do it in the solitude of your own yard, garage, bedroom, or living room. Ready for an awesome challenge? Let's do it!

Forgive Yourself

For many, showing compassion to others comes way more easily than bestowing it on yourself. Maybe you've been judging yourself for a past moral misstep, or are feeling guilty for turning down an invite or setting boundaries at work. It's time to practice a little forgiveness and compassion toward yourself! Here are some easy ways you can let yourself off the hook and keep shame from sabotaging your life:

- **Tell your inner critic to shove off.** That nagging voice in your head that's questioning your every move? It's only serving to bring you down. One way to silence that nag for good is to give it a name and practice cutting it off immediately when it tries to interrupt your day. Try a silly name, like Sarsaparilla, and say "I don't have time for you today, Sarsaparilla!"
- **Remember that no one's perfect.** Holding yourself to impossible standards will always result in the same thing: disappointment. Whether you're anxious about a social situation or something larger, keep in mind that expecting perfection from yourself is a fool's game. It's okay to make mistakes (downright *normal*, actually!), and your imperfections only mean that you're human.
- **Keep moving forward.** Shake off the guilt and worry and push forward in your goals. You can't change the past, but you can decide that today is the day you put one foot in front of the other on the path toward success and happiness.

Relax with a Free Yoga Video

Yoga is one of the easiest workouts to do at home: You don't need any special equipment (besides an easy-to-find yoga mat if you don't have a carpeted space), and it's a piece of cake to follow along with a free online video. Whether you want to work up a sweat with vinyasa flow, or have a more restful restorative experience, digital gurus like Adriene Mishler and Jessamyn Stanley are just a few clicks away.

Listen to a New Podcast

Podcasts are a perfect way to learn, laugh, or challenge your thinking when you're hanging out solo or working on a project with a friend. There's a podcast to suit every interest, and they make a great companion to any at-home activity, from following instructions for a new recipe on a cooking podcast to laughing along to a stand-up routine while finally organizing that messy closet. Download one of dozens of podcast apps to your smartphone (you can also find them on iTunes!) and hit Play. Great places to start include *Radiolab*, *Fresh Air*, *Freakonomics Radio*, and *TED Radio Hour*.

Design a Gallery Wall

Do you have tons of artwork and photo prints sitting around that you're not quite sure what to do with? A gallery wall—basically a giant wall collage—will show off those great images, as well as bring personality to any living space. Pick your wall and your pieces, and get planning! There are lots of handy diagrams online to help you choose the right gallery design for your space. You might also consider getting some pieces reframed to better fit your style. Happy hanging!

Pretend the Electricity Went Out

Phones and other digital screens have taken over so much of modern life, but talking with your friends face-to-face will always leave you feeling more connected than texting and instant messaging. Here's a fun challenge for putting away the devices for a night: Have a make-believe blackout. (If you're really hardcore, you can even turn off your circuit breaker for the evening.) Invite some friends over, turn off your smartphones, build a fort with pillows and blankets, make s'mores in your fireplace (or over a gas stove), and read stories out loud to each other. Savor the candlelight and good company before you have to rejoin the realm of the plugged-in.

Read Tarot Cards

Tiptoe into the world of divination with one of its most popular art forms. All you need is a deck of tarot cards and some basic instructions to get started! Even if you don't believe in the true fortune-telling power of the cards, doing readings on yourself, a friend, or your partner can make for some magical entertainment. So, let's dive in:

1. **First, choose your deck.** Tarot cards come in all styles, from a classic French vibe to modern minimalist versions that can also double as decor. Pick one that speaks to you.

2. **Learn about your deck.** Major Arcana cards reveal truths about big life events, while Minor Arcana cards reveal everyday secrets. The Minor Arcana cards come in four suits (Swords, Cups, Pentacles, and Wands) that represent thoughts, emotions, money, and passion, respectively. You can find out more online, or in the guidebooks that are often sold with tarot decks.

3. **Now it's reading time!** A three-card spread is the traditional style: Draw one Major Arcana card to represent the archetype of the person being read, then three Minor Arcana cards for insights into the fortune of his or her body, mind, and spirit.

Make a Dessert Pizza

Pizza might be one of your favorite dinners, but who says a pie has to be savory? Think outside the (pizza) box by making one for dessert. For a sweet pie, you can fashion the crust from cookie dough, brownie dough, pastry, or anything sugary your taste buds are craving. Then it's on to the fun part: the toppings! Your "sauce" base can be made of jam, caramel sauce, chocolate ganache—whatever calls to you. And to finish it off, the candy jar's the limit; think streusel topping, toffee bits, marshmallows, chocolate chips, or, to make it healthy (well, *more* healthy), fruit. Pizza for dinner *and* dessert? Yes, please!

Read Hilarious Comics on *The Oatmeal*

Matthew Inman was one of the earliest web cartoonists to experience meteoric success. You've probably seen his funny musings on topics like *Facebook* and cat ownership, and the relatable struggles of everything from hangovers to the agony of customer service phone calls. You can easily spend hours going through comics in Inman's online archive and catching up on his latest works. Craving more *Oatmeal* in your life? Inman also sells posters and prints of his funniest works and has developed a book series of new illustrations.

Whip Up Your Favorite Comfort Food

Skipping out on social plans means rejecting pricey restaurant meals in favor of eating whatever *you* want. That's where the concept of comfort food comes in, which means embracing the hearty and filling meals you loved as a kid—like spaghetti and meatballs, macaroni and cheese, meatloaf, and chocolate cake. Did you have an obsession with chicken nuggets? Could you never get enough of cheese pizza? Tonight's the night for satisfying your inner kid by cooking your favorite homemade meal. Savor every delicious, stomach-warming bite.

Watch *Dead Poets Society*

You'll be glad you're at home with the space for a few feel-good sniffles at the emotions of *Dead Poets Society*. This 1989 classic features Robin Williams in one of his most iconic roles. The late actor plays John Keating, an English teacher at an all-boys boarding school who inspires his students through the art of poetry. Keating's challenging curriculum results in some pushback from parents and school administrators, but in the end, nothing can take away the lifelong impact he has on his young students. You'll come away from this acclaimed film motivated to make your own life extraordinary.

Wake Up Earlier

Even night owls can benefit from the increased productivity of an early wake-up call. Make it easier to hit the hay the night before by cutting out caffeine and alcohol at least four hours beforehand, putting your phone out of reach, and doing some meditation before bed. Next, set your alarm for one hour earlier than usual. Getting out of bed might be a struggle at first, but there is joy to be found in the stillness of the world around you before everyone has woken up. Whether you use the time to exercise, make a schedule for the day, or just sip a hot cup of coffee, you'll be surprised how satisfying an earlier morning can be—and maybe even skip that snooze button more often.

Read *Bossypants* by Tina Fey

Fey's 2011 bestseller will crack you up with its sarcastic yet insightful views on life, work, motherhood, and cruise ships. And if you're a fan of audiobooks, you'll love this version, which Fey narrates herself. Other books by celebs that will keep you in stitches are *Is Everyone Hanging Out Without Me?* by Mindy Kaling, *The Misadventures of Awkward Black Girl* by Issa Rae, and *Yes Please* by Amy Poehler.

Design a Tattoo

Permanent body art is definitely something you want to plan out ahead of time. Google ideas, find inspiration on *Instagram*, research tattoo artists in your area, and sketch possible designs for your dream piece of ink.

Challenge Your Brain

Even if it's been years since you took a college entrance exam, or if you never took it in the first place, test your current knowledge and give your brain a workout by taking a free online practice SAT. Compare scores with a friend or partner if you want to add a little friendly competition to it.

Shower with the Lights Off

This is strangely relaxing! Keep a nightlight on or a candle burning (in a safe spot) if you don't want to bathe in total darkness. The dim atmosphere will encourage you to tap into your shower more mindfully with your other senses: the feeling of warm water cascading over you, the relaxing scent of body wash, and the calming sounds of water flowing into the drain.

Do a Paint-by-Number

Paint-by-numbers might make you think of elementary school, when you painted a dog by filling in its nose with one color and its fur with another, but did you know you can create some really cool artwork with paint-by-number kits specifically made for adults? Order one online or download one to print for free, and paint a landscape, still life, or portrait that you'll actually want to frame, hang on your wall, and brag about to guests.

Start a Journal

In today's tech-driven world, it's easy to lose touch with the joy of writing in a physical book. Instead of posting on social media about your day, revive this art and detail your thoughts on paper. Use the space to release your emotions, plot out your work progress, keep track of new ideas, work through a difficult relationship problem, or just freewrite or even doodle. One of the coolest things about journaling is that you'll have a tangible archive of your thoughts and dreams to go back through whenever the mood strikes.

Get Cozy

The Danish people love coziness so much that they've given it its own nomenclature—*hygge* (pronounced "hoo-gah")—and dedicated an entire lifestyle to it. Think winter comfort: soft fabrics, warm and soothing tastes, the enveloping stillness of the evening. Hygge is all about finding joy in the small things in life and in the simple ways of pampering your senses. Here are some ways to bring this snuggly concept to your own home:

- Light a candle
- String up some twinkly lights
- Enjoy a good book
- Put on some big, wooly socks
- Slip into an extra-large sweater
- Decorate your hardwood and tile floors with plenty of soft rugs
- Add natural elements like raw-edge wood tables and real plants
- Wrap yourself in a flannel or cashmere blanket
- Host a small, candlelit dinner party for your closest friends
- Banish overhead lighting by using lots of table and floor lamps
- Light a fireplace and listen to the crackle of burning wood
- Warm your hands on a cup of tea or mulled wine and take deliberate, slow slips
- Splurge on new bedding and pillows

Watch a Puppy or Kitten Livecam

If you don't have a pet of your own, you can still get your cuddly fix thanks to the magic of the Internet. There are tons of sites where you can watch baby animals doing all kinds of adorable things live. On the *Animal Planet* site, you can peek in on puppy and kitten rescues, and on Explore.org, you can get a glimpse of guide dogs in training. Watching cuddly creatures online will ease stress and brighten your whole day.

Build a Blanket Fort

A touch of childlike wonder can turn your own living room into a fun and functional hideaway. Make like a kid and retreat from the world under a big, soft pile of pillows and throw blankets. To set up your cozy oasis, drape some sheets or sleeping bags over the backs of chairs set up in a circle or rectangle. Once you have an outsiders-proof nook, stock it with pillows and blankets, snacks, books or other activities, and even Christmas lights. If you don't trust your family members or roommates not to intrude, underscore your need for solitude with a well-placed KEEP OUT sign. Phew, they're gone! Now you can read, nap, or watch a good video in your cozy hideaway.

Introduce Two Friends

Playing friend matchmaker is a great feeling when they really hit it off. But you won't know until you try! Pick two people you know from different circles in your life—maybe one friend has just moved to a city where another friend lives—and ask each of them if they'd be interested in meeting someone new. If they're both game, set it up over email or group text. Maybe nothing comes of it, or you could catalyze a lifelong friendship between them.

Take a Virtual Museum Tour

You don't need a car or plane or even your own two feet to experience the wonder of a famous museum. Many of the Smithsonian institutions, for example, offer virtual exhibit tours on their sites, so you can zoom and click your way down their halls without leaving your couch. You can tour the moat of the Louvre, wings of the British Museum, and even the ceiling of the Sistine Chapel with only an Internet connection. Happy art-gazing!

Exchange Massages

Professional massages can be expensive (and require, you know, going somewhere), but trading shoulder and back rubs at home with someone you feel comfortable with is both relaxing *and* free. Even a brief massage can relieve headaches and boost energy.

Make Your Bed

Start the day off with an accomplishment by taking five minutes to make your bed. It might seem small, but that's also what makes it a great message to send to yourself: The little things in life can go a long way toward making you feel successful.

Take Online Quizzes with a Friend

Who's more introverted? Who's more likely to snag their crush soon? Who's more like a hamburger and who's more like a hot dog? You can find the answers to all of these questions and more with just a click, thanks to the Internet. Happy quizzing!

Sign Up for a Subscription Box

Having a big box of goodies mailed to your doorstep is like getting birthday presents even when it's not your birthday. Whether you're into cute clothes, hot sauce, sports memorabilia, or makeup, there's a service that will ship a box of whatever you enjoy to your door monthly. Plus, you'll get to try items you might never have discovered on your own; just sign up online and let the treats come to you. A whole new set of socks, wine, or dog toys without having to actually go shopping? Yes, please.

Listen to a New Music Genre

Whether it's nineties alternative, country, or trap music, you probably have your go-to genre locked in. But when's the last time you branched out and listened to something totally outside your comfort zone? You may find some new favorite tracks lurking in an unexplored corner of your music streaming service. Venture into hip-hop, opera, classic rock, EDM, or whatever feels foreign and give it a shot! You just might discover a new appreciation for Tiësto or Led Zeppelin or Justin Bieber.

Give Back

Clamoring to help stop climate change? Want to join the fight for human rights? You can volunteer for and support great causes and charities without leaving the house! Here are some ways to get started online:

- **Raise your voice.** Change.org lets you join others in petitioning for a better planet, and DoSomething.org lets you browse causes and actively get involved with ones that matter most to you.
- **Find your perfect fit.** On sites like VolunteerMatch.org, you can hunt for opportunities to serve your community within your schedule. You'll be able to find a volunteering group that you really connect with.
- **Give your time.** On LearnToBe.org, you can sign up to be an online tutor for a K–12 student, while Catchafire.org connects professionals with opportunities for pro bono work.
- **Donate.** If you're short on time, it's easy to help fund people and organizations online, either via a crowdfunding site like *GoFundMe* or by giving directly to a charity. For example, you can use DonorsChoose.org to donate supplies and electronics to public school teachers for their classrooms.

Host a Black-and-White Movie Night

Choosing to watch a movie in monochrome might feel a bit like opting to get directions from a paper map in the era of GPS, but some of the best films of all time were made before the dawn of Technicolor. Have your friends each bring a classic movie and host an old-school cinema night. Some great film choices: *Casablanca*, *Psycho*, *It's a Wonderful Life*, *Dr. Strangelove*, *To Kill a Mockingbird*, *All About Eve*, and *The Seventh Seal*. Take your party to the next level by having everyone come dressed only in black and white!

Write a Fan Letter

Just because you're a grownup doesn't mean you're immune to the excitement of receiving a real autograph from one of your idols! It's easy to find addresses online for your favorite star's office or P.O. box, and if you include a self-addressed stamped envelope, you might even get a cool memento in return. Take the time to pen an earnest note about what they and their art mean to you. If nothing else, it'll feel good to reflect on how their work has impacted you.

Grow Orchids

These tropical flowers have a reputation for being high-maintenance, but orchids are actually a cinch to grow and will reward you with a lengthy spell of gorgeous blooms. You can snag a mature orchid for an affordable price at a local grocery or plant store, or find bulbs at most greenhouses. Just make sure you keep the plant(s) in indirect sunlight and don't water the roots more than once a week.

Read *Wild* by Cheryl Strayed

Strayed's 2012 memoir of hiking the Pacific Crest Trail hit number one on *The New York Times* Best Sellers list and was later turned into a movie starring Reese Witherspoon. Spend an afternoon immersed in her gripping story of lost love, family tragedy, and redemption in Mother Nature.

Check Out an Online Auction

Score a beautiful antique or a hard-to-find pair of designer sneakers without ever getting up from your couch. With sites like *eBay* and *Poshmark*, you can browse and bid on all kinds of items and maybe even land the perfect deal. You can also sell your own items to bidders.

Try a Tongue Twister

When's the last time you tried to make it through one of these fun linguistic challenges? In the seclusion of your own home, no one can hear you recite "Peter Piper picked a peck of pickled peppers" and "I saw a kitten eating chicken in the kitchen!" over and over again until you feel like your tongue is tied in actual knots. Find an online list of classic tongue twisters and see how many you can do in a row. Start by saying each one slowly, then try to repeat them faster and faster, and see if you can improve with practice.

Make Tasty Fruit Kebabs

All-natural fruit kebabs are such a fun way to get your vitamins in! Just skewer the fresh fruit of your choice on a wooden stick and dip it into yogurt mixed with vanilla and honey for a healthy, refreshing snack. To step up your kebab game, try:

- Cutting the fruit into fun shapes like hearts and stars
- Making rainbow kebabs (strawberries, cantaloupe, pineapple, green grapes, blueberries, purple grapes)
- Mixing cocoa powder into your dip for a chocolaty snack
- Adding marshmallow or cream cheese to your dip for a more desserty taste

Watch A Star Is Born

There are four editions of this classic Hollywood musical film out there. Marathon them all (or at least two or three) and decide which *Star* is your favorite. Here's a mini guide to the films:

- **The original 1937 movie.** Starring Janet Gaynor and Fredric March, this version narrates the story of Esther, a woman aspiring to Hollywood fame, who gets her wish when she meets a renowned but troubled actor, Norman.
- **The 1954 musical.** With a different screenplay, this second version stars Judy Garland as Esther, and was released to great critical acclaim.
- **The 1976 musical.** Barbra Streisand takes a turn in the spotlight, playing opposite Kris Kristofferson (Elvis Presley was briefly considered for the role as well). This version was the third-highest-grossing film of the year.
- **The 2018 film.** Bradley Cooper directs and costars alongside Lady Gaga in the most modern remake, which was nominated for Best Picture and produced the smash hit song "Shallow."

Have a Lucid Dream

Lucid dreaming means being aware that you're dreaming *while you're still asleep*. Some lucid dreamers even find they have the power to manipulate the outcome of their own dreams as they occur. You may have experienced this surreal phenomenon by accident in the past, but did you know that you can take steps to actively trigger a lucid dream? There are several tactics that lucid dreamers share online, but one of the most powerful is repeating a mantra of intent, like "I am going to have a lucid dream," to yourself as you fall asleep. Give it a try!

Take a Mental Health Day

Sometimes a day off from work or school is just what you need to heal your spirit. Whether you're struggling with feeling burned out or just haven't had a day to yourself in a while, there's no shame in using the sick time you've been given to focus on relaxing and rejuvenating. Spend the day in the yard or on the porch enjoying nature, or stay in doing whatever you please. You'll return feeling like a better version of yourself—ready to tackle whatever comes next.

Design a Vision Board

A vision board is a physical manifestation of goals you want to achieve. Close your eyes and imagine your dream career or home, or a personal goal, like learning to love yourself more. Then, set yourself up for success by creating a tangible visual of that aspiration. Here's how:

1 Set the mood with some inspiring music.

2 Pause for a moment and reflect on your goal to set an intention for your board. What is the goal? Why is it important to you? What would it mean to you to achieve that goal?

3 Clear a physical space to work in and gather your supplies. You'll want some old magazines or access to a computer with a printer. For your actual board, you can use a posterboard, corkboard, or other large, flat surface.

4 Locate images that connect to your goal and give you inspiration: a favorite movie character that resonates, a quote that motivates you to keep plugging away, etc.

5 Pause with each found image for a moment, and if it feels right, affix it to your board.

6 Once you've filled up most of the space on your board, sit back and reflect on it as a whole. How do you feel when you look at it? Does it empower you and bring you joy? Keep adding and changing things until you've created a powerful reminder of your goal.

7 Prop up or hang your board somewhere you'll see it often.

Learn Origami

Did you ever learn to make a paper crane in school? Not all origami (the traditional art of Japanese paper folding) is that complex—or that simple, if you're interested in a challenge. Using online tutorials, you can fold all kinds of shapes to fit your fancy; all you need is a sheet of paper! When you get the hang of it, you can also buy special origami paper in all kinds of textures and prints. Origami is a great hobby to keep your hands busy. Plus, you can make special gifts for friends and family!

DIY an Escape Room

An escape room is a physical adventure game where you and a group have to solve a series of puzzles in order to "escape" from a confined space. The problem is, they can be pretty pricey. Stretch your creative muscles by making your own escape room at home for a group of friends or family members to try out. Make up a story: Did your group get locked in a museum overnight? Maybe they need to escape from a mad scientist's lab? Create some riddles and set a time limit. Hopefully your group can escape before the time runs out!

Host a Crock-Pot Cook-Off

Have a few friends bring over their slow cookers and make a fun contest out of dinner. Who can make the tastiest chili or stew? Who has the best macaroni and cheese recipe? Use the time while dinner is cooking to catch up on each other's lives, then sit down to a warm meal together!

Read *The Underground Railroad* by Colson Whitehead

Immerse yourself in a story so gripping you'll forget all about the outside world. Colson Whitehead's 2016 Pulitzer Prize–winning novel follows the story of two slaves in a bid to escape from a Georgia plantation. Whitehead's gift for storytelling culminates in an ending that will stay with you long after you're finished reading.

Evaluate Your Carbon Footprint

Are you making efforts to carpool or take the bus instead of driving every day? Are you using LED or other energy-efficient light bulbs? Are you recycling? Take stock of your carbon footprint (EPA.gov has a great free calculator to help you out) and consider ways you could live a little greener.

Refresh Your Home with Aromatherapy

Between the dirty laundry, pet odors, and dust, the air in your home can get a little stale—or downright unpleasant. Keep your pad cozy and inviting by making sure it smells fresh. Here are a few tricks for a great-smelling space:

- **Get an essential oil diffuser.** With just a few drops of lavender, lemon, or eucalyptus, your whole home will be transformed.
- **Clean out your fridge and trash cans.** Sometimes we can overlook the most obvious sources of funky odors. Toss everything in your fridge that's past its prime, but also remember to give the shelves and drawers a good scrub to get rid of any lingering spills and stains. Also wash the insides of your trash cans.
- **Send moisture packing.** Humidity breeds mold and mildew, which can trigger allergies as well as bring unwanted odors into your closet, basement, or bathroom. Invest in a dehumidifier or inexpensive crystal moisture absorber like DampRid. Also make sure to regularly wipe down your shower curtain and bathroom walls to keep your space mildew-free.

Get Ordained

The traditional path to ordination usually requires years of school—not to mention sizable tuition payments. But thanks to technology, you can become an ordained minister over the Internet in a few simple steps (and no student loans!). With ordination through the online Universal Life Church, you can legally officiate a friend's wedding in most states. And don't worry if you're not particularly devout; many venues for online ordination don't require commitment to a specific religious tradition. If nothing else, you'll have a great "fun fact" to break the ice at any social event.

Laugh at Funny Comics on Xkcd.com

Garfield is a classic, sure, but sometimes you want a cartoon that really taps into your nerdier side. Enter *xkcd*! Created in 2005 by Randall Munroe, a former physics student and roboticist, this long-standing web comic cracks jokes on topics like science, computer programming, and math that any academic can relate to. His signature stick figure cartoons also manage to make profound insights about life along the way. New comics come out on Mondays, Wednesdays, and Fridays, so check back in whenever you want an instant mood-booster. You'll laugh, learn something, and maybe have your mind completely blown.

Have a Good Cry

You'll feel better—really! Though some people may still label crying as something "weak" or "too emotional," research shows that tears actually have a lot of great health benefits. Crying can improve your vision, strengthen bonds between two people (when crying in the company of another person such as a friend or romantic partner), and even elevate your mood by releasing stress hormones. Spiritually, it can feel amazing to unleash your emotions in a physical way. So, let it out without apology. Your body and mind will be grateful.

Join a Fantasy Sports League

You might think you have to be a total sports buff to play in a fantasy league, but the beauty of fantasy sports is that you can draft teams at random and still have a shot at winning the whole shebang. You can find a league through a friend or colleague, or join one at random on an online fantasy sports site. With fantasy sports, you get the rush of cheering for your favorite teams without having to, you know, go out to actual games.

Have a Nineties Rom-Com Marathon

Grab a flannel and some tissues: The nineties were a golden era for charming, whimsical, and just plain fun romantic comedies. Even if you've seen many of them before, they never get old. So go ahead and relive a time when Doc Martens and mini-backpacks ruled the fashion realm, and actors like Hugh Grant and Sandra Bullock seemed to open new movies every other month. You'll get a kick out of the cheesy plot points and seeing now-obsolete technology like dial-up Internet. (Hey, it worked for Tom Hanks and Meg Ryan!). Invite a few friends over if you choose, and make sure they dress the part too. Here are some classics to get you started:

- *Clueless*
- *Notting Hill*
- *10 Things I Hate About You*
- *You've Got Mail*
- *Never Been Kissed*
- *Pretty Woman*
- *Reality Bites*
- *Shakespeare in Love*
- *While You Were Sleeping*
- *Four Weddings and a Funeral*
- *Sleepless in Seattle*
- *My Best Friend's Wedding*

Start a Garden

Even if you don't have a large outdoor space to plant to your heart's content, you can start a tiny plot of flowers or vegetables in your backyard or in some containers on the porch. Watching plants sprout from seeds and nurturing them as they grow will enhance your connection to the natural world.

Read a Comic Book

Don't be intimidated by comic books if you've never read one before! They're the perfect medium for relaxing in your favorite chair and getting lost in a good story. Try starting with a classic series, like Superman from DC Comics, or Archie from Archie Comic Publications, Inc. (comics aren't just for superheroes!), or ask for recommendations at your local comics shop next time you're out. You can also try a popular graphic novel like *Watchmen* by Alan Moore and Dave Gibbons or *Blankets* by Craig Thompson.

Juice Up Some Homemade Lemonade

All you need is lemons, sugar, ice, and water to whip up a big pitcher—or a single refreshing glass—of cool lemonade.

Fight Off Gloomy Days with a Sun Lamp

The frigid temperatures, limited sunlight, and short days of the colder months can make anyone feel blue—especially those who are prone to seasonal depression. Light therapy via a sunlight lamp is one simple way to help shake off those gloomy vibes—it promotes the regulation of feel-good hormones like serotonin and can reset your sleep-wake cycle. You can find a natural-light lamp in your price range on sites like *Amazon*. Turn it on the next time you're feeling down to make your home a little happier.

Watch *The Marvelous Mrs. Maisel*

This smart and at times deeply emotional show by the same talented writer that gave us *Gilmore Girls* (Amy Sherman-Palladino) will suck you into the exciting, difficult, and altogether unpredictable world of a woman in stand-up comedy in 1950s New York City. You'll fall in love with Miriam "Midge" Maisel, the outgoing, hilarious socialite whose life is soon turned upside down. Be careful, because once you start your viewing, you'll be up all night telling yourself, "Just one more episode."

Dream Big

What would you do if you couldn't fail? Sit down in a quiet, comfy space in your home and take some time to get in touch with your goals and dreams. Think in terms of the year ahead, but also beyond that. What do you want to achieve in your career, love life, personal life, and even your role in the larger world? You don't have to decide on all of your goals right now, but practice reflecting on the bigger picture and figuring out what steps you can take today to get what you want in the long term. It will make your big dreams that much more attainable down the line.

Make a List of Free Things to Do in Your Area

Maybe you're usually content with laying low on the weekends, but then there's that one sunny Saturday where you wake up and think, I should *do* something. While you're snug at home now, use your time to research all the things you can do in your own neck of the woods when that mood strikes next. Your list can include things like free museums, hikes and nature walks, outdoor festivals, bookshops and libraries, and other local attractions.

Relax Your Jaw

You can carry a lot of tension in your jaw and facial muscles without even realizing it. Consciously take note of and then release stress in your mouth, tongue, and jaw to feel calmer.

Listen to ASMR Videos

ASMR, or autonomous sensory meridian response, is a tingling sensation that people may get when listening to specific sounds, like a whispering voice or the tapping of fingernails on marble. For many, ASMRs can calm anxiety and help them relax. To see if it works for you, look up a few videos on *YouTube*, close your eyes, and let the sounds move you.

Throw a Board Game Party

Jump back into a decade past by hosting a nostalgia board game party for your friends. Ask everyone to bring their favorite games, and plan out which ones will be played when. You'll have a blast reliving your years as a kid whose main stress in life was reaching the end of Candy Land.

Feng Shui Your Space

The ancient Chinese art of arranging your space in a spiritually pleasing way can make your pad an even cozier place to call home. Take a shot at incorporating some of these feng shui options in your favorite rooms and see if it improves their vibe:

- **Add plants for color and air clarity.** Jade plants, ferns, and bonsai are all feng shui–approved to bring good energy into your space.
- **Decorate with all five Chinese elements.** A balance of these five traditional principles (fire, earth, wood, water, and metal) will unify a room and promote harmony within it.
- **Keep the front door of your home clean and bright.** Stop going in through the garage or the back door and utilize the front entryway, which represents how qi (energy) enters your life.
- **Keep curtains and blinds open to let the sunshine pour in.** Light is essential for the flow of qi.
- **Nix clutter.** Mess in your space will drain your energy; tidiness buoys it.
- **Keep your toilet's lid closed and the bathroom door shut.** Water represents money, so seal your bathroom to prevent money from draining away.

Make a Scrapbook

In a time when photos exist mainly in the digital cloud, printed pictures can feel extra special. Capture your memories in a way that transcends social media by putting together a physical scrapbook. Print out your favorite photos from over the years and organize them by year, geography—or however you decide—then decorate each page with stickers, fancy lettering, and other fun scrapbooking elements. When you're done, you can keep the scrapbook for yourself or gift it to a family member.

Put Your Phone on Airplane Mode

Social media notifications, new email alerts, group texts: Who needs all that around the clock? You definitely *don't* need these intrusions sapping your attention when you're trying to enjoy the present moment alone. Develop a stillness ritual by silencing your phone for a few hours each day, or at least overnight. There's nothing selfish about taking a break from the digital drumbeat and recharging with help from the blissful quiet of an offline device. You can catch up when you sign back on.

Read *The Power of Now* by Eckhart Tolle

Everyone wants to spend more time living in the present moment instead of dwelling on the past or fretting about the future. But that's easier said than done. Tolle's recommendations are informed by a number of different spiritual traditions and focus on slowing down, connecting with nature, and reducing anxiety caused by things that are out of your control. His book will help you fight FOMO and re-center your mind on the present.

Massage Your Trigger Points

You can treat your own muscle aches and pains—and those tense knots known as trigger points—with a little self-massage. Rolling out your back with a tennis ball can release back pain, and just thirty seconds of pressure on your temples can help relieve headaches. To find treatments that work for you, consult with a doctor or physical therapist, or find a routine through a trusted online source or book.

Conquer an Intimidating Board Game

Has Risk always left you scratching your head? Have you aspired (at a distance) to be a Settler of Catan? Sometimes the most rewarding pastimes have a higher barrier to entry than your typical board game. There's no time like the present to finally take on that seemingly inscrutable game! Invite your most fun-loving friends over and tackle the challenge together. There's no instruction book too dense to be cracked with the help of some good snacks and good pals. You might even discover a new favorite.

Go On a Guilt-Free Unfollowing Spree

Social media can be a great place to keep up with your friends' lives and post about your own—but it can also be a huge drain on both your time and your spirit. You might have those friends who post too much or post only negative things, or acquaintances you haven't talked to in ages who update their followers on things you honestly don't care about. Don't feel any shame about muting or unfriending anyone whose posts are constantly making you feel down or insecure, or who you will likely never reach out to in a direct message. Life's too short to waste on things that don't lift you up, so purge whoever you need to from your social media feeds. It's a vital act of self-care.

Say No

Summoning the power to turn someone down—and not feel guilty about it—is up there on the list of hardest things for most people to do. Maybe a friend invites you to happy hour and you're not really feeling it, but you go along anyway. You might feel you have to have a "valid" excuse ("Oh sorry, I'm having dinner with a friend!") instead of just saying you want to have a quiet night at home. Brushing aside your desires, you end up feeling worn out.

So how do you overcome the guilt and finally learn how to say no? Here are a few tips:

- **Identify your needs.** How frequently do you need alone time to keep your emotional battery at a good level? How long do you typically enjoy being out before you start to feel ready to go home? Are there any factors that can shorten or lengthen that time (who you are with, what you are doing, etc.)?
- **Set boundaries.** These should focus on the needs and social limitations you identified above.
- **Take it in smaller steps.** Start by declining an invite with a simple "I'd love to, but I have plans!"—without including that your plans are to just eat dinner and go to bed. Over time it will get easier to turn down plans without automatically giving a detailed excuse, until finally you are able to just say "No thanks!"

Remember: You don't need to justify your need to take a pass on a social outing. "No" is a complete sentence.

Read *Pride and Prejudice* by Jane Austen

Use a night in to lose yourself in a classic love story. The famous Mr. Darcy courts a skeptical Elizabeth Bennet in Austen's renowned 1813 novel. More than just a romance, *Pride and Prejudice* is a study in wit, the trappings of wealth, and well-rounded character development. When you're done, watch one of the BBC film adaptations or the 2005 version starring Keira Knightley.

Start an Herb Garden

Did you know you can grow some of your favorite cooking herbs like parsley, sage, and chives indoors? All you need is a window that gets plenty of sunlight (a south-facing one is best), some clay or plastic pots that have room to drain, good potting mix, and your seeds. You should start seeing sprouts in two to three weeks!

Awaken the Force with a Star Wars Marathon

Invite a group of friends over, or go it (Han) solo, and binge the original trilogy to get your fix of Ewoks, Princess Leia, and the lovable adventures of R2-D2 and C-3PO. And if you dig the prequels, put on those as well for an out-of-this-world weekend marathon.

Trace Your Family Tree

Have you ever been curious about your genealogical roots? Or wondered which part of China or Poland your great-grandparents immigrated from? With the Internet at your fingertips, tracking down your ancestry has never been easier! You can use sites like Ancestry .com to map generations and find the names of your ancestors going back *centuries*. There are also sites that let you look up recorded histories of different families. For a more in-depth look at your own biology, order a DNA test from a site like 23andMe.com to test your genetics and connect with living relatives from around the world.

Create a Private Reading Nook

Reading is the perfect way to shut out the real world for a hot sec and dive into an exciting, romantic, mythical, or even scary adventure. So why not make sure you're *physically* cloistered from interruption during this time too? Set yourself up for prime coziness by making a little reading sanctuary in your home. Choose your comfiest chair, set up a table nearby for your book, a drink, and maybe a plant to add some life. If you want extra privacy, hang some curtains or set up a folding screen so you can be completely alone with your book. Your future reading time will feel like a genuine escape from the rest of the world.

Plan a Vacation

Thanks to the Internet, you can sate your wanderlust without ever leaving home. Even if your travel budget is currently a bit scarce, it doesn't hurt to dream! You might end up with a solid vacation plan, but if not, you'll have a fantastic trip to add to your ultimate bucket list. Here are some vacation elements to help jump-start your game plan:

- **Your fantasy place to stay.** Check out a home-rental site like *Airbnb* or *Vrbo* to find options in the location you've always dreamed of visiting. A castle in the Irish countryside, a sleek urban loft in Los Angeles—a faraway country, or a domestic destination: The world is yours for the traveling!
- **Your favorite travel method.** From first-class flights to a road trip in a vintage convertible, you have tons of transportation options for your ultimate holiday.
- **Your ideal itinerary.** Whether you're an adventure junkie or more of a drinking-wine-on-a-patio type of vacationer, get a head start on activities in your destination of choice by looking up popular attractions, guided tours, and treks you can do solo.
- **Your dream dining experience.** A lot of the fun of vacation is that calories don't count, right? Maybe you fancy an elegant omakase in Tokyo, or overstuffed po'boy sandwiches in New Orleans. Look up restaurants and bars along your journey and plan what you'd eat and drink.

Order Groceries Online

These days, you can skip the long lines at the market and have your food delivered to your door with the push of a button. Sign up for a service like Instacart or Shipt, and get all your favorite snacks to your doorstep without having to put on real pants.

Light a Candle

Nothing is more soothing than a favorite scent and a gently flickering flame. And if you're into DIYs, you'll be happy to learn that making your own candles at home is a breeze. All you need is a wick, some wax to melt, and scented oils. You might soon be on the way to starting your own candle business.

Bust a Move

It's time to live out the motto "Dance like no one's watching." Even if your best move is "the sprinkler," boogying around your kitchen and living room to your favorite beats will get your heart rate up, stretch out those muscles, and most importantly, make you smile.

Do Yoga Breathing

In just twenty minutes (or less), you can use your own breath to fend off anxiety and find calm, thanks to yoga breathing. To do this exercise, first find a quiet space in your home. Next, breathe in deeply through your nose as you silently count to six, then exhale slowly and gently out of your mouth for another six count. Repeat until you feel relaxed and refreshed, working your way up to lengthier intervals for each inhale and exhale. You can also add variations or new techniques if you choose. You'd be surprised by the effect a few minutes of intentional breathing can have on your spirit.

Make a Care Package

Distance doesn't have to isolate you from the ones you love. Use the power of gifts to make a faraway friend's day! Pack a big box full of baked goods (homemade or store-bought), toiletries, candles, fun games, books they might enjoy, or other treats. Include a personal note, send it off, and imagine the smile on their face when they open up your box of goodies. It's thoughtful gestures like these that can truly bring the most meaning to the lives of you *and* your loved ones.

Plan Your Halloween Costume

The September costume panic is *real*. If you procrastinate on choosing your Halloween look until the last second, you risk ending up with something seriously shoddy—or worse: a tired cliché. Get a (pirate) leg up on the holiday by planning your costume ahead of time. Do you want to go as a movie character? A creative pun? Will the costume be homemade or store-bought? You'll have plenty of time to shop online for the right accessories, or craft your own ensemble, and you'll avoid a last-minute drive to the costume store for that last uninspired look remaining on the shelf.

Watch *Forrest Gump*

Spending a couple of hours with Tom Hanks is always a good choice. In this 1994 classic, Hanks plays a charming Alabama man who has a profound effect on the world around him. You'll be won over by Forrest's straightforward kindness and his perseverance. You'll also hear the origin of some of the most quotable movie lines of all time, like "Life is like a box of chocolates. You never know what you're gonna get" and "Stupid is as stupid does." You'll laugh, cry, and take in the simple pleasures of life with a renewed sense of magic.

Read Life of Pi by Yann Martel

Hunker down for a thought-provoking day with Martel's 2001 classic adventure fantasy. *Pi* stars Piscine "Pi" Patel, an Indian boy who survives a shipwreck in the Pacific Ocean—in the company of a Bengal tiger. When Pi's parents hire a ship to transport their family and various zoo animals from India to Canada, everything goes wrong. Alongside the major themes of perseverance and individuality, Pi's ecumenical approach to his faith gives him a unique lens through which to view both his world and his journey for survival, culminating in two different accounts of what happened to him while adrift in the ocean.

Life of Pi has sold millions of copies and won a ton of prizes, including the Booker Prize for Fiction in the United Kingdom. And if the title sounds familiar, you might have heard of the 2012 movie, directed by Ang Lee. Watch the film after you've read the book for an even deeper dive into Martel's narrative, and compare the two!

Make Your Own Papier-Mâché Volcano

If you never made one in school, you'll be surprised at how simple and fun it is to create your own mini "erupting" volcano. Papier-mâché paste can be made out of just flour and water, and all you'll need for the volcano itself is an empty twenty-ounce soda bottle, some newspaper, and your imagination. Baking soda and vinegar colored with red food coloring will make the volcano "erupt" in an exciting lava effect.

Turn Off Your Phone

When's the last time you actually turned your phone completely off? Even if you already mute your phone before bed, take it one step further and power it down all the way before hitting the hay. It'll prevent you from checking in on social media both when you're trying to fall asleep and if you wake up in the middle of the night. In the morning, see how long you can wait before powering it back on. Turning off your phone can also help extend the battery life, so take a full break from your screen for the sake of your mind *and* your device's longevity.

Read Satire

In between reading real headlines, you might need a break from all the doom and gloom in the world. Lighten your mood by switching to some humorous "current events" from the creative minds behind some of these sites:

- **The Onion.** The Internet's favorite satirical newspaper, *The Onion* does a great job of skewering modern events and revealing idiosyncrasies in just a few words.
- **Reductress.** A dry and witty take on traditional women's magazines and their often alienating articles, *Reductress* was founded by comedians Beth Newell and Sarah Pappalardo. It skewers topics like dating, beauty, and women's friendships with on-the-nose satire. It also pairs each post with a funny photo.
- **ClickHole.** *ClickHole* is actually from the creators of *The Onion*, and it shows: The site parodies those "clickbait"-style content links you find all over the Internet and social media. With its hilariously weird slideshows and absurdist takes on personality quizzes, you'll laugh over *ClickHole*'s content as you recognize the familiar formats they mimic.

Watch Manatees Cozy Up Underwater

There's nothing more soothing than watching these giant, gentle mammals bob up and down in the waters outside Florida's Manatee Lagoon. And thanks to their live webcam, you don't need to hop on a plane to see it for yourself! The manatees are easiest to spot between November and March.

Have Sex

While the feel-good effects of sex are, well, pretty obvious, sex also releases important hormones that are good for your physical health. Studies have found that regular sex can lower your blood pressure, boost your immune system, improve your sleep, and even help you lose weight. As if you needed any more incentive!

Learn How to Play Chess

Don't let chess intimidate you. Sure, it can involve a lot of strategy at advanced levels, but you can also have fun just learning how each piece moves, or challenging someone to a match if you already play. Plus, playing chess sharpens your analytical skills, memory, and discipline. If you're having a solo night, you can play chess against a computer or virtual stranger in a free app or online.

Host a Karaoke Night

Karaoke bars cost money and mean abandoning your comfy living room—so bring the magic to your home. Buy an inexpensive karaoke machine (or a karaoke game for a console you may already have), invite a few friends over, and have a blast belting out your favorite hits. (Actual singing skills are optional, because karaoke should be more about having fun than putting on a flawless performance.) If you don't want to invest in an actual machine, and don't have a console compatible with the different game versions, you can pull off the same effect with *YouTube* lyric videos and the power of your own lungs.

Roll Out Muscle Aches

It hurts so good! Foam rolling your sore muscles can feel a little uncomfortable at first, but all that pressure is helping you do a myofascial release on your trigger points, stretching tight muscles and helping you recover faster from exercise or injury. Start off with your iliotibial (IT) band by lying on one side and placing the foam roller under your hip. Gently roll back and forth, bringing the roller from your hip down to your knees and back. Do a few passes while breathing deeply until you feel some release, then switch to the other side. Once you master IT band rolling, you can move on to other parts like your back, glutes, and quads.

Make Homemade Dumplings

Mmm, dumplings. Not only is a pillow of dough stuffed with savory or sweet fillings totally tasty, but it is pretty much a universal cuisine. Every culture has its own version, from pierogies, momos, and wontons, to bao, ravioli, modak, and samosas. Pick your favorite dumpling version to make from scratch and cook up a delicious, filling feast. Of course, while making everything homemade guarantees the most authentic flavor, you can also take a shortcut by using premade fresh or frozen dough. Pair your creations with plenty of traditional sides and sauces for a well-rounded and hearty meal.

Cue Up a *Friday Night Lights* Marathon

This five-season drama about high school football in Texas would hit even the toughest person you know right in the feels. In the cult favorite that fans rescued from the brink of cancellation, Coach Eric Taylor and his wife, Tami, must tackle their new, challenging roles as football coach and high school principal, respectively, while also contending with tough issues like poverty, failure, and family dynamics. Even if you're not the world's biggest football fan, you'll chuckle at the Taylor family's antics, sob at their regrets, and get hooked on the Dillon Panthers' trials and tribulations.

Write or Call Your Senator

Do your part for democracy by voicing your stance on issues that are important to you. No matter how you feel about the executive leadership in your country, legislators are in power to be a voice for their constituents—and that includes you. Here's how to reach out:

- **Choose a congressperson.** Even if you're sure you know, verify! You can find your senators on Senate.gov, and locate your House representative by submitting your zip code on House.gov.
- **Plan your message.** Explain in your letter why you're reaching out. Go into detail about your beliefs, and close with the action you'd like them to take. Strive to be thorough but concise! If you're going to call, plan a loose phone script of talking points to get your thoughts across well.
- **Mail it or call.** If you're writing, email or snail mail both work. For phone messages, look up your legislator's office directly, or call 202-224-3121 for the main Capitol switchboard. Be sure to include your name and address in your letter or phone message, because mail from actual constituents is more likely to be passed along to your representative.

Give Yourself Permission to Be Lazy

Between work and personal demands, those pesky, unavoidable errands, and trying to have a social life, it seems like everyone's always on the go. And it's easy to feel guilty if you're not busy 24/7 too. But if you don't take time to give your brain and body a rest, you run the risk of burning out. The next time your friends invite you to barhop across town, or you see a crowded party going down on *Instagram*, give yourself a firm, verbal pass to skip it and recharge by doing absolutely nothing. Sometimes all it takes to squash guilt is that direct reassurance! When you're ready to hang out again, you won't be burning the candle at both ends.

Reread Your Favorite Childhood Book

Sure, you've grown past the target market for *The Very Hungry Caterpillar* and *The Giving Tree*, but that doesn't mean these stories are any less meaningful to you now than they were when you were a kid! Find a copy of your favorite book from decades past and enjoy flipping through it again. Think back to how it made you feel when you were younger. You might discover some of the magic you once cherished in the story is still there.

Slow Down with the Five Senses

Stress affects your body in both mental and physical ways. When your mind can't slow down, your heart rate and breathing attempt to keep pace, leading to feelings like panic and dread. And as you play that game of keeping up with your thoughts, it takes a toll on your body, causing anything from headache or muscle pain, to upset stomach or insomnia.

If you start feeling tense about the future, an easy way to calm your mind and body is to take a deep breath and go through the following mental list, pausing to really reflect on each question:

- What do I see right now?
- What kind of sounds do I hear?
- What are my fingers touching? What is the texture like?
- What do I smell?
- What do I taste on my tongue?

Take a few more breaths after reflecting, and feel as your body relaxes and your thoughts are pulled back to the present. By focusing on what you're sensing in the current moment, it's hard to keep a grasp on those worries about the future.

Brew Your Own Beer

If you love all things ale, making your own beer at home is a fun activity that also keeps you from having to hit up a loud, crowded bar. You'll just need to order a few home brewing tools, along with brewer's yeast, hops, and grains online. You can also find prepackaged kits with everything you'll need. Who knows? Maybe there's a brewery job in your future.

Read Your Horoscope

Whether you're a hardcore astrology buff or you just like the entertainment of predicting the future, dive into the latest forecasts for your sign. You can find your horoscope online, or download an app on your smartphone that will give you regular updates.

Watch *Silver Linings Playbook*

Dramatic yet funny, this award-winning 2012 film stars Bradley Cooper and Jennifer Lawrence as seemingly opposite people who enter a dance competition together. Themes of mental illness, romance, and the power of family make this a gripping story for any movie fan.

Do a Home Improvement Project

If you rent, you can stick to a simple task like putting up temporary wallpaper or changing out your plain showerhead with a fancier one. If you own your place, the ceiling's the limit! Think painting an accent wall, overhauling your bathroom sink, or even getting to work on a major kitchen renovation. And thanks to *YouTube*, there are countless free online tutorials to help you tackle your projects—big or small. By investing time in bettering your living space, you'll reap the benefits for months (or years!) to come.

Start a Social Media Account for Your Pet

When the pressure of human social media starts to drag you down (always need those perfect pics and killer captions!), switch over to a much simpler—and cuddlier—profile by making your dog, cat, or even fish the star of the show. Post cute videos of them doing tricks or just looking cute, follow accounts of similar pets, and interact with other animal lovers. If nothing else, you can use the account as a digital photo album to collect every adorable moment in your pet's life.

Read *The Prophet* by Kahlil Gibran

A monumental work of spiritual fiction, Gibran's collection of poetic essays is one of the most critically revered books of the last century. His insights into everything from marriage to prayer—via a protagonist who's just returned to his homeland after twelve years in exile—will move you. You'll also recognize selections that are frequently read at weddings. *The Prophet* has been translated into more than seventy-five languages—plus it entered the public domain in January of 2019, which means you can find a free copy online!

Learn How to Change Your Car Oil

One of the most inevitable tasks you face in car maintenance is changing the oil. So why not take some time to learn how to do it yourself? By DIYing this routine job, you'll save money, learn a ton about the machine you drive daily, and impress all your friends with your skills. And don't stress: It's as simple as draining the old oil into a pan, slipping in a filter, and adding the new oil. There are tons of videos online to help you out. Never again will you have to spend three torturous hours waiting in line at the mechanic's shop!

Host a Book Club

Want to read more and also hang out with your favorite people—without leaving your cozy home? Start your own book club! As the bibliophile in charge, you'll have control over the length, expectations, and tone of your meetings, like whether to go with strict page count requirements or keep the vibe more casual. Here's how to get your club off the ground:

- **Decide on a genre.** Fiction? True crime? Self-help? Graphic novels? It's your club, so the whole Dewey Decimal System is your oyster.
- **Choose a book.** Are you going old-school classic or new best-seller? Hardcover books can be expensive, so factor cost into your decision. Bonus points if people can check out the book at a library.
- **Send invites.** You'll want to be judicious about how many people you invite to your club, since more than ten members can make discussions more challenging.
- **Choose a regular time and day.** Ask members which days and times work better for them, and plan accordingly.
- **Plan the snacks.** This might be the most important part! Is your club a fancy tea and scones venue, or is it more of a wine club that happens to read occasionally? Make it potluck-style so everyone has a chance to contribute and no one is breaking the bank.

Watch Stand-Up Comedy

Skip the crowded clubs and two-drink minimums and get your comedy fix online by streaming a routine of your favorite comedian. You can laugh out loud and never worry about strangers spilling beer on you or blocking the view.

Order an *Etsy* Print

Browse talented artists and order a print of your favorite saying or song lyrics from one whose style speaks to you. Hang it somewhere you'll see it regularly.

Preset Your Morning Coffee or Tea

It's a small step, but prepping your morning beverage the night before makes getting out of bed that much easier. Think of how awesome it'll be to wake up to the smell of your coffee already brewing before you even stumble out of bed.

Start a Blog

Think of it like an online journal where you can control the look, content, and readership. Choose a service that makes creating and keeping up on your blog easy, like Medium.com or WordPress.com. You can anchor the content around a certain topic you are interested in—cooking, fishing, or college, say—or write up a storm about whatever's happening in your life that day. Another great thing about a blog is that it's searchable, so you can quickly find different keywords and topics to reread what you wrote. Plus, it can be as public or private as you'd like; if you'd rather write just for yourself, you can publish anonymously, or set the posts to be viewed by you only.

Schedule Alone Time

Make sure you get your regular dose of rejuvenating solitude by actually penciling it into your schedule ahead of time. The same way you allot time for meetings and doctor's appointments, designate time for relaxing and tuning out the rest of the world, whether it's through a 7 a.m. meditation or an 8–10 p.m. reading session. Once you've set your alone times, hold them sacred—just like those other important appointments—so nothing comes between you and your self-care.

Build a Ship in a Bottle

It's a timeless hobby that always has people scratching their heads and asking, "How did that ship get in there?" And now you can be the one to create an "impossible bottle" puzzle that will stump all your friends. Check out easy-to-follow instructions online and collect the tools needed to get cracking on your own sailing sculpture! For advanced bottle puzzles, try your hand at inserting a tennis ball, a deck of cards, or a Rubik's Cube.

Diffuse Lavender Oil

Aromatherapy is a simple, all-natural way to lift your mood, help you relax, and even catch some quality zzz's. Lavender in particular has been shown to alleviate symptoms of anxiety and depression, as well as combat insomnia. To reap the benefits, spritz your pillow with diluted lavender essential oil, apply a few drops to your wrists, or diffuse it through your home with an essential oil diffuser. If lavender isn't your first choice of soothing scents, you can try sandalwood or chamomile, both of which also encourage better sleep.

Make Your Own Cleaning Products

Baking soda, vinegar, essential oils, and an empty spray bottle: That's all you need to whip up your own household cleaners! When you DIY your own cleaning products, you save cash *and* get a fresh-smelling home, without using a bunch of noxious chemicals or waiting in line at the store. So when you run out of that store-bought cleanser (or ahead of time, to save the last-minute mad dash), skip the trip to get more and look up an easy recipe for a glass, all-purpose, or bathroom homemade spray instead. You'll also be able to incorporate your favorite scents, like lemon and rosemary!

Have a Paper Airplane Battle

You can turn a paper airplane contest into a very serious lesson about the principles of aerodynamics if you choose, or you can just have a ton of fun pummeling your friends with mini jets constructed from sheets of an old notebook. If you want to try a distance contest instead of full-body combat, measure the length of everyone's throws from a set starting point, or have an airtime contest by using a phone timer to measure how long each plane stays aloft. But if you *would* rather fight it out, grab some scrap paper and start folding. There's no time to talk: This is war!

Construct Your Own Sushi

What's great about sushi restaurants: beautiful rolls, chilled sake, and great ambience. What's not so hot: the price, and having to put on something other than sweatpants. Making your own sushi at home is inexpensive and a ton of fun! You just need three different ingredients that you can have delivered to your door the day of, or buy at the market ahead of time:

- **Sushi-grade raw fish.** If you can't find sushi grade, you can always stick to vegetarian sushi like avocado or California rolls.
- **Cooked rice.** Nishiki rice is a popular choice for sushi. Add some seasoned rice vinegar for that sweet and tangy flavor!
- **Nori (seaweed).** Find thick sheets that won't break when rolled.

Next, you'll want to use a thin bamboo kitchen mat to help roll up the sushi once you've layered the rice and toppings on your nori. Slice your roll into pieces with a sharp knife, and you're ready to eat! Serve with plenty of soy sauce, wasabi, and pickled ginger. You might never want to leave the house for sushi again.

Binge Episodes of *Friends*

By now you've probably caught at least one episode of this classic nineties sitcom about six friends surviving New York City life together. There are ten seasons all together (that's 236 episodes!), so you have plenty of opportunities to crash on the Central Perk couch and get to know Joey, Rachel, Ross, Monica, Phoebe, and Chandler—or catch up with them after some time away. And though it's worth settling in to catch every joke, *Friends* is also the perfect show to have on in the background while you do things around the house.

Snuggle under a Weighted Blanket

Anxiety sufferers swear by weighted blankets, which are designed to ease stress and help you drift off to sleep faster through the calming sensation of being hugged. The perfect blanket for you should weigh between 8 and 10 percent of your body weight, and you can even get a cooling version designed to prevent overheating while you snooze. Order one online to give the soothing effect a try for yourself. Warning: You might never leave the house again once you've experienced *this* degree of complete relaxation.

Say Ten Things You Love about Yourself

Come up with at least ten compliments for your wonderful self, then stand in front of a mirror and say them out loud in a confident voice. You might feel silly at first, but the empowering effects of this easy activity are immediate! You'll soon be going about your day with an extra spring in your step.

Watch *Do the Right Thing*

Use your time inside to watch one of the best and most provocative films of all time. Set in Brooklyn, this 1989 Spike Lee film tackles big themes like racial tension, and delivers a powerhouse soundtrack.

Discover New Music

It's super easy to fall into a rut of listening to the same twelve songs every day. But thanks to the recommendation system built into streaming services like Spotify and Apple Music, finding great new tunes has never been easier. The next time you're tempted to fire up the same tired playlist, change it up by finally giving those suggestions a chance.

Choreograph a Dance Routine

Have you always secretly wanted to be a backup dancer for Janet Jackson, or thought you'd do a bang-up job showing off your stuff in a music video? Maybe you've never choreographed for Beyoncé, but you can still invent your own dance moves to a killer track. Pick your favorite song to bust a move to and craft your own steps. (If you need a little help, *YouTube* has a full library of choreography ideas!) If you're feeling brave, show off your routine to a fellow fan.

Teach Your Pet a New Trick

Okay, maybe your pet will never star on Animal Planet, but did you know that even cats can learn basic tricks? Assess your pet's learning abilities by starting with the basics like sit and shake. If they're already further along than that, go for a crowd-pleaser like roll over. You'll boost your pet's general aptitude for obedience and bond with them on a deeper level by improving your communication. And if you don't have a pet, make a friend happy by offering to help train their dog!

Create a Closet-Cleaning Ritual

Freeing your closet space of old and unwanted items will not only open up physical space; it will also make your mornings so much easier. Get into a minimalist mind-set by whittling your wardrobe down to the essentials with this process:

- **Put on your favorite music.** Get those energy levels up and get ready to clean!
- **Drag everything out of your closet space.** Yes, *everything*—even those seasonal items.
- **Decide what makes sense to keep.** Some helpful criteria: Would you wear that item tomorrow (or when it was in season)? Does it fit well? Does it make you feel confident? Arrange separate piles for things to keep, donate, or toss (damaged or extremely worn items).
- **Donate what you don't want.** Pack up the discarded items and drop them off at a thrift store or a shelter or charity of your choice.
- **Organize what's left.** Use bins, drawers, and hangers to ensure you can easily find different items when you're getting ready in the morning.

Now you can bask in the clarity of your new, uncluttered closet!

Read the Harry Potter Series

The Harry Potter books are the ultimate hole-up-at-home adventure! These seven engrossing fantasy novels make it totally easy to lose yourself in the magical world of Hogwarts. Whether it's your first time meeting Harry and his friends, or your copies are well worn, immerse yourself in the magic of quidditch, spells, and mythical creatures. And after your book binge, a movie marathon awaits; stream all eight movies for even more Pottermania.

Write a Letter to Your Future Self

Who will you be in one, five, or ten years? Where will you be? What do you want "future you" to remember? To have done? Pen all these thoughts in a letter to yourself for the ultimate time capsule. You can write your letter on paper and put it in a safe location (or give it to a family member) to save for the future. Or use a site like FutureMe.org to create a digital version that will be emailed to you at a specific date in the future.

Laugh Your Way Through The Office

Decide whether you want to watch the American or British version (or both!) of this hugely popular comedy series. Steve Carell and Ricky Gervais, respectively, star as the bumbling bosses who manage teams of quirky characters. You can find episodes for free on streaming services including *Netflix* and *Hulu*. The top reasons why *The Office* is worth tuning in to:

- **Relatable workplace humor.** If you've ever fantasized about pranking an annoying colleague, you'll live for Jim's cheekily antagonistic relationship with Dwight.
- **Relationships that will make you laugh and cry.** From Jim and Pam's journey as coworkers to something more, to Oscar and Angela's dynamic friendship, *The Office*'s true strength is in showing how work colleagues can become family.
- **Lovable characters.** When you think of sitcoms, you might not often think of complex, unique characters that you feel truly connected to. *The Office* does a terrific job of developing sincere, relatable personalities you'll feel like you know in real life. Seeing Michael Scott evolve from a clueless manager to genuine friend might just tug your heartstrings.

Hone Your Crossword Game

Between the daily puzzle in your local newspaper and books full of crossword collections, you'll never run out of options with this fun mental workout. It also makes for a great competition with a friend or partner. If you're feeling bold, use a pen!

Treat Your Feet

Here's an easy way to get spa-quality soft skin while you sleep: Coat your feet with a generous amount of your favorite lotion, then put on a pair of chunky socks. Next, tuck yourself in to bed, and wake up with softened calluses and happy toes.

Go On a Shopping Spree in Your Pajamas

Being cozy while shopping for more cozy things—is this heaven? Scour the Internet for onesies, flannels, lounge pants, oversized tees, and any article of clothing that makes you want to curl up indoors for as long as possible.

Hang a Bird Feeder

Make sure it's just outside a window so you can watch the birds flutter by all day. You'll spot the differences between a blue jay, swallow, robin, and cardinal—and maybe get a little obsessed with your bird community's natural feeding rhythms. Plus, watching birds nibble up birdseed is surprisingly soothing. Start with a basic window feeder and some traditional black oil sunflower seeds and see who stops by for a snack. Want a larger variety of feathered friends? Mix up your seed types to attract a more diverse population, or court a certain species. A hummingbird feeder is easy to keep stocked with sugar water that will draw striking little hummingbirds to your window.

Teach Yourself a New Language

Learning a foreign language can seem challenging as an adult when you don't have AP French homework to keep you honest, but thankfully, technology makes it fun and easy. Download a free smartphone app like Duolingo or Memrise and start learning Spanish, German, French, and more—without having to leave your *casa*. By spending even a few minutes each day on word exercises, you'll be on your way to becoming fluent in a whole new tongue (or at least able to ask "Where's the bathroom?" in several of them).

Film Your Own Cooking Show

Have you ever dreamed of being the next Emeril? Do you love imagining an audience is following along when you whip up a recipe—even if it's only ramen? With your smartphone camera, you can record yourself teaching someone how to make your favorite recipe, or racing to create a perfect cake. And it's okay if it never sees the light of *YouTube*!

Here's what you'll need for your cooking show:

- **A concept.** Will you walk your audience through a recipe, like an old-school Martha Stewart show? Or have a competition with a friend to see who can make the fastest, best-tasting filet mignon?
- **The right equipment.** If you want to branch out from the smartphone, you can get high-tech with a professional camera. A tripod will also keep your shot steady and capture every detail of your delicious dish.
- **Video editing software.** You might get through everything on the first take, but even so, you'll want to add fun graphics and captions to your video. Try an app like Adobe Premiere Rush or LumaFusion, or a computer program like Adobe Premiere Pro or Corel.
- **Your ingredients and cooking equipment.** Can't forget the most important part of a cooking show!

Watch *The Shawshank Redemption*

Do you feel like expanding your mind—without changing out of your pajamas? Make your couch time more meaningful by taking in one of the best dramas of all time. Set in Maine, this 1994 film follows the journey of a man (Andy Dufresne, played by Tim Robbins) sentenced to two consecutive life sentences for the alleged murder of his wife and her lover. With themes of forgiveness, friendship, and unlikely bonds forged in unexpected places, *Shawshank* will make you think more about the roles of justice and rehabilitation in society.

Have an At-Home Date Night

Who needs restaurant waiting times and loud moviegoers when you can rev up the romance in the comfort of your own space? Charm your other half by thinking outside of the typical dinner-and-a-movie date. Some ideas:

- Set up a scavenger hunt
- Draw funny portraits of each other
- Order desserts from your favorite restaurant
- Have a water gun fight outside
- Make a mini wine bar by putting together a charcuterie plate and a wine tasting
- Work together to write the story of how you met

Build a Terrarium

A garden that you don't have to weed or water obsessively? Yes, please! Terrariums are one of the easiest plantscapes to both build and maintain, and they'll add a gorgeous dose of green and constant source of joy to your living space. Here's what you'll need to make your own:

- **A clear glass container.** It can be as large as a wide-bottomed planter, or as small as a reused salsa jar. Get creative! You can also use a wine bottle, a cookie jar, or a glass ornament if you want to make a hanging terrarium. Open terrariums—like a cookie jar with no lid—are great for growing succulents, whereas closed terrariums, like one inside a sealed jar, are more conducive to plants that require humidity, like ferns.
- **Small rocks or sea glass.** These will be laid down as a base layer for your terrarium.
- **A hearty soil, like potting mix.** This will be the next layer, taking up half of the jar's space.
- **Your plants.** Tiny succulents and moss work great.

Plant away! For some final artsy touches, you can add small figurines, little pieces of driftwood, or anything that will make your terrarium feel more you. To maintain your terrarium's vibrant look and to stimulate growth, spritz it with water every other week. Enjoy your earthy, low-maintenance decor!

Listen to a Favorite High School Album

Were you obsessed with Nirvana as a teen? Couldn't get enough Britney Spears or No Doubt? Go back to a simpler time when bills were just something parents complained about and music was a formative part of your identity, by revisiting your favorite musical artist, album, or track. Even if hindsight makes you realize your most cherished song of the time wasn't actually all that great, it's still powerful to see how music can take you back in time and make you feel like you're reliving your youth. Bonus points if you can find the original CD and listen to it on your old CD player or boom box.

Find a Pen Pal

Corresponding with someone across the country—or world—might not only open your mind to new perspectives; it can also be the foundation for a lifelong friendship. Because you're removed from your normal social circles, you'll feel free to be your authentic self in your letters. And you can keep connecting with them even if you move to a new home or get super busy. (Just write at your own pace!) You'll grow a tangible archive of conversations that you can treasure forever. So, how do you find your long-distance friend? Sites like *PenPal World* make it a snap to connect with people across the world who have similar goals and are keen to talk with someone like you. And of course, getting real, non-junk mail (even email!) is always fun.

Give Someone a Hug

Did you know that hugging releases feel-good hormones, passes on the restorative power of human touch, and lowers blood pressure? Wrap your arms around someone special to do a free good deed— and reap the benefits for yourself.

Make a To-Done List

To-do lists can be stressful. Instead, make a list of things you've *already* done. You can look at it and instantly feel successful—even if the only things on it are "brushed teeth" and "took dog for a walk."

Hang Up a Hammock

What's more relaxing than literally hanging out in the shade on a sunny day? If you're lucky enough to have a backyard with two perfectly located trees to hitch to, invest in a hammock so you can nap outside with reckless abandon. But even if you don't, you can always take one to a nearby park, or set up a standing hammock— no trees required!

Paint with Watercolors

Watercolors are the perfect medium for painting amateurs: "Mistakes" like bleeding and oversaturating can still create beautiful works. You can start with a few inexpensive paints and brushes purchased online, and work your way up to professional-quality equipment if you find yourself passionate about this art form. Try your hand at brushing out some simple shapes or ombré patterns, and even attempt a landscape once you've gotten more confident. Then, master fun techniques like blending and shading. You can use your new skills to hand-paint wedding invites or place cards, or just make some bright paintings to decorate your space with.

Give Yourself a Back Massage

If you own a tennis ball, you own a cheap, portable, and effective massage tool! Lie down on a comfortable surface like a yoga mat or rug and place the ball between your back and the surface. Roll your body back and forth and in circles on the ball, guiding it over spots where you have muscle tightness. The gentle pressure will help relieve tension in these areas. You can do this self-massage whenever and wherever you're feeling an ache.

Play a Round of MASH

A classic fortune-telling game that stands for "Mansion, Apartment, Shack, House," MASH is something you might have played in grade school. But just because you've outgrown the days of lockers and school crushes doesn't mean you can't have fun looking into your future! All you need is a pen, a piece of paper, and a friend.

1 Choose what categories you'll be predicting for the future. (Maybe start with the classic big three: 1. Partner, 2. Number of children, and 3. Car you'll drive.)

2 Have your friend list four options for each category. Write these all down and put the letters *MASH* at the top of the page.

3 Have your partner close their eyes while you start drawing a simple spiral, then ask them to say "stop" at a certain point as you are drawing.

4 Count the number of rings in the spiral. That's your magic number!

5 Starting with the *M* in MASH, count each item in a category until you get to the magic number. Cross off each option you land on until one is left, then repeat with the remaining categories.

6 Read your partner's destiny aloud. Then it's your turn!

Light Incense

Let the soothing smell and gentle smoke of your favorite Nag Champa or palo santo incense fill your home! Incense does more than just give your space a great aroma; it can boost creativity, lift your mood, and help you tap into a more spiritual or reflective mind-set. It comes in several forms, like sticks, cones, and resin, so pick the one that's best for you and light it up. Use the peaceful atmosphere to do some yoga or meditation, relax, or just go about your day.

Make a Vegan Version of a Favorite Recipe

Your favorite dish could taste just as good, or even better, without any meat, dairy, or other animal products, plus it's a great challenge for your culinary skills! To veganize your recipe of choice, there are tons of tried-and-true substitutes, like switching margarine for butter, agar-agar powder for gelatin, and almond milk for cow's milk. You can also find tons of recipes online for nondairy mac and cheese, black bean tacos, "chik'n" sandwiches, and vegan versions of pretty much anything that tickles your taste buds. Give one a whirl; you just might find that chickpea "tuna" salad tastes better than the real thing.

Lose Yourself in a Daydream

Have you considered the healing power of spending a little time with your head in the clouds? Daydreaming may be something you were discouraged from doing as a kid, but it is now being discovered as a great way to focus on your goals and let your creativity inspire new ones. Turn off your phone, sit in your favorite chair, and give your mind permission to wander. Turn your attention inward and resist the urge to plan or think about your day. Instead, let your mind travel to larger dreams, like the promise of a new job or home.

Try Parkour

Parkour—a French obstacle course–style type of acrobatics—not only looks cool, but is also a great form of exercise you can do anywhere, including your own digs. Advanced parkour, like jumping off of tall walls or scaling staircases, takes a lot of training and involves important safety precautions, but as a beginner, you can learn basic body weight movements at home. Use an online guide or video to safely practice moves like balancing and small jumps.

Start a Compost Bin

Instead of throwing banana peels, coffee grounds, and fruit and vegetable scraps in the garbage, you can put a lot of your food trash to work for the planet! Composting uses natural decomposition to break down your organic waste into fertile soil. First, check to see if your municipality takes compost. If yes, you can then simply deposit your food waste in provided bins. If not, you can make your own compost heap in your backyard or even in your kitchen with a special bin. In time, you'll have rich, composted soil to enrich your garden.

Binge *Breaking Bad*

Go ahead and get comfy, because you've got five seasons of this AMC smash hit to enjoy. Bryan Cranston's famous turn as Walter White, a high school teacher who turns to producing and selling meth to fund his medical treatments, drew critical acclaim and a huge cult following. Aaron Paul also stars as Jesse Pinkman, White's affable former student, now partner. Thrilling and also heartbreaking—and culminating in one of the best finale episodes of all time—this drama is the perfect binge-watch for late nights.

Go to Bed Early

Ending your night early can make all the difference in the morning; you'll wake up feeling rested and ready to start the day off right. To fall asleep earlier, banish screens in the bedroom and read a book or listen to a relaxing podcast to wind down before bedtime.

Tackle a List of Movies "Everyone Should See Before They Die"

Skip the high-priced theaters and work your way through one of these lists of classics from a site like *IMDb* or *Complex*. By the end, you'll be well versed in the history of cinema—and have a better appreciation for the genres you already know and love.

Play Darts

You might have played for fun in a dive bar, but do you know that the game of darts has official rules? Get a hold of an old dart board and play different versions with a partner, or work on your skills solo. It's probably safer to lob darts at home than in a crowded bar, anyway.

Make a Homemade Pizza

It's quick, it's customizable, and you don't have to do so much as call the pizza place or answer the door for a delivery person. You can buy a premade crust, or make your own dough from scratch; pizza dough is one of the easiest to make, so don't be intimidated! For sauce, a classic marinara will do nicely, but you can use anything from pesto to barbecue sauce. Add your favorite cheeses—a mixture of shredded mozzarella and fresh mozzarella balls will give you that perfect melted gooeyness of the slices from your go-to pizza joint. To finish it off, grab pepperoni or sausage, fresh peppers, onions, shrimp, shredded chicken, or whatever toppings are calling your name.

Write a Short Story

Looking for a fun challenge? Try creating a captivating narrative in five hundred words or less (or even just two hundred if you want to go all minimalist). The key to telling a satisfying story in a small space is structure: Have a clear beginning, middle, and end. Start with a compelling hook to get your reader engrossed and to establish what emotions are at stake. Next, choose words carefully to make the most of your limited space. If any portion of your story doesn't advance the narrative, cut it. Finally, wrap up with a powerful ending. You don't necessarily need to tie a neat bow on the plot, but definitely try to leave the reader with a strong emotion or thought that sticks around long after they've finished reading.

Have a Screen-Free Day

From *Netflix* to iPhone games, electronic screens have truly usurped the fight for our attention spans. Can you even remember the last time you weren't reachable via one device or another 24/7? Think back to a pleasant time in the past when you were off the grid. Maybe it was a family vacation in nature, or a concert you went to as a teen where people weren't recording on their phones all night. Picture how free and blissful it would feel to cultivate that stillness in your life once again.

The magic of being disconnected is only a few off switches away! To recapture the serenity of the days before you carried an instant Internet connection in your pocket, spend a day (or weekend) sans all devices, and see how living the no-screen life affects your mood. Go hiking, boating, or exploring your city—or just relax at home with a good book, fun craft, or cooking challenge to keep you company. Resist the pull of social media, whether it's scrolling through your newsfeeds or posting about your activities. At the end of your off-the-grid time, check back in with yourself. How do you feel? You might be inspired to regularly schedule a no-screen day in your calendar.

Watch *Legally Blonde*

When you're staying in, you don't always want to watch hours of a TV series, or a movie that takes a ton of concentration and interpretation. Enter *Legally Blonde*! This extremely quotable 2001 rom-com tells the story of Elle Woods, an L.A. sorority girl who tries to win back her ex-boyfriend by enrolling alongside him at Harvard Law School. Plot-wise, the movie mirrors a typical love story—at first. Then, things take a few unexpected turns. You'll laugh at Reese Witherspoon's hilarious performance as Woods.

Get Virtual Book Recommendations

You might have felt that very specific emotion of finishing a great book and being both excited...and also mildly depressed because the story's over. So what to read next? Luckily, it's never been easier to find a new read perfectly tailored to you. On WhatShouldIReadNext.com, you can type in the name of a book or author you like and match with tons of great recommendations. It's like having a librarian on speed dial. Enjoy your new reads!

Soak Up a Loving Memory

Feeling stressed or anxious can make it impossible to really unwind during a day in. Practice mentally unclenching your fists with this antianxiety trick: Take a few deep breaths in and out, and summon a memory of a moment when you felt truly loved. Keep breathing, and recall the warmth you felt in that moment—how big your heart felt, and the feeling of a smile pulling across your face. Notice how your mind and body start to relax as you travel through this memory. Use this exercise whenever an anxious thought comes knocking!

Learn Calligraphy

Looking for a fun but also inexpensive hobby? Try calligraphy! And don't worry if your handwriting isn't the greatest: You don't actually need tidy penmanship to make elegant letters. All you really need is a calligraphy pen, some paper, and simple instructions. A great way to start is to download a calligraphy practice worksheet online that lets you trace over letters until you feel confident enough to try it freehand. As you gain more skill, you can experiment with different brush strokes and colors, and try your hand at writing longer sentences. And if you get really good, you can even put your new talent to use by doing lettering for a friend's wedding invitations, or selling your wares on *Etsy*.

Watch a Spelling Bee

Test your brain power by streaming a past spelling bee online and pausing to see if you can correctly spell different words. You might gain new respect for the contestants!

Create Your Own Tea Blend

Maybe you have a favorite tea already, but when you mix and match different varieties of loose tea, you can create a blend that's uniquely you. Oolong and lemon ginger? Earl Grey and lavender? Peppermint citrus? There are so many options! Order some tea online and have fun customizing your next steaming cup.

Make Room for Productivity

Tidy space; tidy mind. Spend some time cleaning your home workspace by recycling any paper waste, wiping down your desk, organizing all those paper clips and scissors, and generally making the space a little more streamlined. The next time you sit down to knock off some work or pay some bills, you'll thank past you for the extra elbow room.

Quilt

For a craft that will help you live your coziest life, arm yourself with an array of fabric scraps or old T-shirts, get some batting to stuff with, and start quilting! Free quilt patterns are available online so you can find a design that speaks to you and get to work on your custom bedspread. A sewing machine will make your process faster and more seamless, but you can also hand sew. Not only will you feel super skilled once you've made your own quilt, but it can also make an incredible and sentimental gift.

Find Your Dream Real Estate

Ranch in Montana? Beach house in Malibu? Penthouse in New York? Yurt in the Sierra Nevada? Throw budgets to the wind and surf Zillow.com for your ultimate fantasy home. Thanks to the modern-day marvels of digital real estate, you can window-shop without getting up from your chair, and scroll through dozens of photos to get your snooping fix without having to trek to an open house. Take your time sifting through places to find your absolute favorites, and compare choices with a friend if you choose.

Do a Virtual Act of Kindness

Doing good doesn't always require physical labor—or even leaving your home. You can make someone's day without ever getting up from your computer! Here are some ideas for ways to give back from right where you are:

- Leave a glowing comment on one of your favorite writer's articles
- Send someone an anonymous positive email
- Email a friend or partner telling them why you're proud of them
- Donate to a charity drive on social media
- Pen a sincere recommendation on LinkedIn.com for an old colleague
- Forward email coupons or discounts you receive to others who might use them
- Let someone know if you really enjoy their social media feed
- Donate to a crowdfunding cause
- Send a friend or family member an e-gift card for coffee
- Promote a small business you love over social media
- Join an online forum to foster community with others

Travel Back to Your Childhood

Whether it was sledding on your favorite hill on a snow day or the time your dog got into the Thanksgiving turkey and you had to order pizzas for dinner, take some time to let your mind wander back to the good ol' days before jobs, taxes, and other "fun" adult things. Savor the moments you spent with your family, or recall the memories you made with friends at school. If you have kids, make sure to tell them about your childhood so they can feel connected with your family's history. Plus, they'll love hearing about all the times you embarrassed yourself!

Watch *Jiro Dreams of Sushi*

Go behind the scenes of one of Japan's most famous sushi restaurants in this 2011 documentary that profiles eighty-five-year-old Jiro Ono, a sushi legend and the owner of Tokyo's legendary Sukiyabashi Jiro. In this dreamy account, Ono approaches sushi with the eye and heart of a trained craftsman truly passionate about his work. Immerse yourself in Ono's realm for the next couple of hours and you'll see why people wait years to get into his three-Michelin-star, ten-seat restaurant. Order in some sushi to enjoy during the film too; otherwise, you're sure to come away hungry.

Listen to *Oprah's SuperSoul Conversations*

You really can't go wrong with Oprah. And if you miss her iconic talk show, you'll love this chance to relive some of her classic conversations, and also hear live tapings of new ones. In her first-ever podcast, the "Queen of All Media" interviews thought leaders like Michelle Obama, Eckhart Tolle, Anne Lamott, Gloria Steinem, Lin-Manuel Miranda, and more. It's the perfect podcast to put on in the background while you clean or cook, or when you just want some guidance for wrangling life's biggest questions. Let Oprah's soothing voice transport you to a world of new knowledge.

Read a YA Novel

Just because some books were written with teens in mind doesn't mean adults can't totally relate to the drama. Many young adult (YA) books tackle big themes like mental illness and sexual assault, while others let you just dive into romance for a few hours to escape the rest of the world. Devote a little quality time to the touching stories and heart-pounding drama in a popular title by Rainbow Rowell, John Green, Sabaa Tahir, Kami Garcia, or Suzanne Collins. When you're done, gift the book to a niece or nephew, or a YA-loving friend.

Get Hooked On *Doctor Who*

Can you believe *Doctor Who* has been gracing TV screens since 1963? If you aren't familiar with the plot, the Doctor is a time-traveling alien (masquerading as a human) who explores all dimensions of the universe using a phone box–shaped ship called a TARDIS. The role has been played by thirteen different actors over the years, including the first female Doctor (played by Jodie Whittaker) in series eleven. That's a lot of TV to catch up on! Install yourself on the couch and get a binge-athon going with the Doctor of your choice.

Brew a Fancy Coffee Drink

Skip the Starbucks run *and* save cash by making your own latte or Frappuccino in your kitchen. Grab the milk of your choice, steam it, and mix with different amounts of espresso for a latte, cap-puccino, macchiato, or caffè Americano. And if you have a milk frother, you can froth up a little to top off your treat. Experiment with chocolate syrup for a rich mocha Frappuccino, or peppermint extract for a peppermint latte. If you don't have a fancy machine, you can make ersatz espresso by just brewing some extra-strong coffee!

Host a Fondue Party

What makes fondue a great dinner for guests isn't just how yummy it is (but that helps): It's easy, cheap, and doesn't require constantly hovering over your oven or clearing a ton of plates at the end of the night. Plus, a communal meal means a great community.

To keep things simple, have two large fondue pots, each with one course: a melted cheese entree and a chocolate dessert fondue. For the first, mix a melt-worthy cheese like Emmental with some beer or white wine (or apple cider or chicken broth for an alcohol-free version) and serve up with plenty of bread cubes, vegetables, cooked meat, and apple slices. For dessert, melt the chocolate of your choice to pair with fruit, little squares of pound cake, pretzels, marshmallows, and mini cookies. Make sure your guests have plenty of white wine or fancy sparkling water to pair with their food and enjoy the sitting-around-the-campfire atmosphere of feasting on fondue. (Except the campfire is made of delicious gooey cheese!)

Make a DIY Face Scrub

Even if you wash your face regularly, your skin can still get dull and flaky from dead skin cells piling up. Exfoliating gets rid of that lifeless skin and reveals all of the fresh, vibrant skin cells below the surface, giving you a natural glow. To exfoliate the natural (and cheap) way, try a simple face scrub recipe that will leave you smelling divine and your pores feeling refreshed. You can use your favorite essential oil to lend a custom aroma to your recipe. Then, just spread it on your face and leave it for a few minutes, wash it off, and bask in your glowing complexion.

Watch The Lord of the Rings Series

You can successfully shut out the mortal world with a marathon of the beloved LOTR films, which track hobbits, elves, and wizards on an epic journey created by the magical mind of J.R.R. Tolkien. All three movies are packed with truly amazing special effects and costume and makeup designs, and they star an award-winning cast, including Ian McKellen and Cate Blanchett. The whole trilogy will take you 558 minutes to watch—that's 9.3 hours! So grab your favorite blanket and movie snacks, and settle in for a full day on Middle-earth.

Do a Body Weight Workout

You don't need special dumbbells or weight benches to build muscle and tone at home. Just search online for body weight workouts that use your own strength to give you a solid, full-body workout routine. Typical body weight exercises can include planks, burpees, wall sits, lunges, and crunches. The bonus of exercising at home? You can do it whenever it's convenient for you, whether that's 5 a.m. or 11 p.m. Plus, you can work a routine in while watching a favorite show or waiting for the dryer to be done.

Blow Bubbles

There aren't enough bubbles in adulthood. And did you know you can make your own with water, dish soap, and corn syrup? If you don't have a bubble wand handy, just make your own out of wire or a mason jar ring.

Take a Power Nap

A nap that is too long or too short can leave you feeling groggy or cranky. To maximize your nap time, aim for ten to twenty minutes, which will make you feel more refreshed than a two-hour nap that has you waking up asking "Wait, what day is it?"

Make Homemade Play-Doh

You don't have to be a kid to get a kick out of turning colorful lumps of dough into a beautiful sculpture (or something like that). All you need is flour, water, salt, cream of tartar, and some food coloring to make your own Play-Doh at home. Once your dough is rollin', grab some cookie cutters or silverware to cut and design shapes and release your inner artist.

Spend Quality Time with Hemingway

Ernest Hemingway's famously terse writing style and universal themes make his fiction accessible even decades later. Start with *The Sun Also Rises*, which is considered one of his best, and see if you can make your way through to *The Old Man and the Sea* and *A Farewell to Arms*. As you go, keep a look out for how Hemingway characterizes the Lost Generation (people who came of age during World War I) and how he develops the Hemingway code hero—a hard-drinking and stoic masculine protagonist who proves his machismo through tests of will.

Paint Your Bedroom a Fun Color

Apple green, robin's egg blue, coral pink: The right color can make your bedroom come alive and feel so much more like a custom oasis. If you own your space, there's nothing stopping your paint experiment, but even if you rent, many agreements just require that you repaint any painted walls back to white when you move out. Browse and order paint samples online so you can choose the perfect hue that suits you, and spend a weekend transforming your sleeping space into something a little livelier.

Look Up Random Facts

Sure, having *Jeopardy!* levels of book knowledge can get you far in life. But it's also fun—and makes for a good party trick—to stock up on some totally useless information. Did you know that the combination of an exclamation point and a question mark is called an *interrobang*? Or that 7 percent of Americans think chocolate milk comes from brown cows? Or that you're always looking at your nose and your brain just chooses to ignore it? Scour the Internet for fun facts that you may never get asked on a test but will delight friends and family.

Minimize Social Media Time

Social media has a lot of benefits: It keeps you connected to long-lost friends and can give you a sense of community when you feel adrift. But it can also sap the importance of in-person relationships and make you feel inadequate when you see friends out living it up—even if you were perfectly content with your book-and-tea night before deciding to check in. If you're interested in cutting down the time spent scrolling through your social feeds, here are some easy tips:

- **Post less.** Putting content into the world means you'll be caught in an endless cycle of checking in to see comments and likes. Cut it off at the source by limiting how often you post.
- **Set a strict time each day to check your feeds.** It can be ten minutes of *Instagram* during the hour before you start to wind down for bed, or fifteen minutes to check *Facebook* during your lunch break. If you really struggle with opening your apps on autopilot, hide them in a folder or even delete the apps so you have to log in on a web browser each time.
- **Track your usage and adjust accordingly.** Tools like Apple's Screen Time calculator send you weekly updates on how many minutes you've spent in different apps. If you notice a particular social media app sapping a lot of your attention, schedule a break, or even deactivate your account for a bit.

Update Your Resume

Take some time now to freshen up all of your accomplishments, even if you're not in the market for a new job. When the time comes, you'll be glad you kept everything up to date. Want an entire resume makeover? A resume consultant will edit and reformat yours for a small fee. You can also download a digital resume template for free.

Make a Rug Out of Recycled T-Shirts

It's a great way to make use of old T-shirts that you don't wear anymore but also feel too sentimental toward to donate. All you need is a cheap doormat, a hot glue gun, scissors, and eight to ten old shirts. Then, just cut the shirts into small strips, knot them, and glue them to your mat. When you're done, you'll have a cute new rug and some free closet space too.

Watch *The West Wing*

Even if politics aren't quite your jam, you'll quickly become obsessed with this Aaron Sorkin drama about life in the White House. Martin Sheen stars as the engaging President Josiah Bartlet for seven marathon-worthy seasons of Washington chaos. And don't let the political themes put you off; it's the perfect show for getting comfy in your living room all weekend.

Make Pancakes

Looking for a super satisfying breakfast—or dinner (no judgment!)?
Enter one of the all-time best ways to consume carbs: pancakes.
You probably have all the ingredients in your kitchen already (flour,
baking soda, eggs, and milk), so no grocery store run needed.
Though they're tasty, pancakes also offer healthy minerals, including calcium, fiber, and iron. (So they're basically like a kale salad,
right?) Cook up a big batch and serve them drizzled with real maple
syrup, smothered with fresh butter, and topped with your favorite
fruit. Mmmmmm.

Clean Out Your Sock Drawer

When you shop for clothes online, you probably don't think about
browsing for a new set of funky socks or comfy boy shorts. But
nothing feels better than a brand-new pair of the items you wear
the most! And your socks and underwear store microorganisms
much faster than other clothing, making it even more important to
replace them regularly. Take a tough eye to your sock (and underwear) drawer. Toss anything that's tattered or threadbare—even
that beloved pair of socks with cats eating pizza on them that has a
big hole in the toe—then order some fresh ones online.

Dive Into Astronomy

You don't need a science degree or fancy equipment to see stars millions of miles away! Orion is one of the easiest constellations to spot; just keep an eye out for those three stars lined up in a row to form the mythological Greek hunter's belt. From there, you can spot tons of other constellations and planets—and with just a pair of binoculars, you can inspect craters on the surface of the moon. You'll find worlds of information online for astronomy buffs and beginners alike, from informational books to apps that map the sky for you. You can even look into getting a telescope if you do want to take your stargazing to the next level.

Try a Meal Delivery Kit

What's way better than schlepping out to the grocery store? Having everything you need to make a delicious dinner delivered directly to your door! Blue Apron and Plated are just two popular services that ship recipes and prepackaged ingredients right to you, making cooking your own dinner a breeze. Plus, you'll never waste another minute on that daily "What should we have for dinner?" quandary. You just might be tempted to nix shopping at the grocery store altogether!

Design Your Dream Menu

A farm-to-table feast of dim sum delights? Ice cream for all three courses? Give your taste buds a chance to dream by planning out the food offerings for your own fantasy restaurant.

Discover Your Hogwarts House

Do you know if you're more Ravenclaw than Hufflepuff? Or a tried-and-true Gryffindor? In just a few minutes, you can sort yourself into your proper Harry Potter Hogwarts house on Pottermore.com. When you're done, you can compare houses with a friend!

Smile in the Mirror

You might feel silly at first, but try it! Taking a second to see your own smiling face can boost your confidence and lift your mood—no selfie required. You can even add a positive affirmation by telling yourself a compliment or an empowering mantra.

Make Your Own Kombucha

This fermented tea packs a big probiotic punch and a delicious, slightly sour taste. To make your own, you'll first need to make or acquire your own SCOBY (symbiotic culture of bacteria and yeast), which functions as a starter for your kombucha and will need to set for about one to four weeks. You can purchase SCOBY online separately, or as part of a kombucha starter kit. How-to videos and instructions for making your own can also be found online. Once you've got your SCOBY, all you'll need is tea, sugar, water, a large jar, vinegar, and a little patience as your kombucha ferments over two weeklong fermentation phases. When it's done, you'll be so proud of your homemade "booch"—and save so much money on store-bought products. Plus, your SCOBY can last for years if you properly maintain it.

Fall Asleep to a Soothing Sound

Many people have trouble getting to sleep. It can be tough to quiet those racing thoughts or tune out outside sounds, no matter how desperate you might be to catch some zzz's. A white noise machine can help filter out background noises that keep you up, but if you're looking for a cheaper and immediate way to get to sleep, there are many free sites that play relaxing sounds. Ocean waves, rainforest ambience, a whirring washing machine: You can find the perfect playlist to conk you out pronto.

Adopt or Foster a Rescue Pet

Every year, millions of pets are waiting in shelters for their forever home. And one of them could be your new best friend! Adopting gives these wonderful animals a new chance at a full and vibrant life—and gives you a rewarding, loving companion. A rescue pet will bring you daily joy and endless snuggles.

Of course, adopting a dog or cat in need is also a big commitment. If you're interested in a rescue pet, and have the lifestyle and time to create a loving home for one, you can check out available animals online at shelters and rescue groups near you. If you're not ready or don't have the time for a full commitment just yet, you can also help by fostering a rescue animal (caring for them temporarily until they find a home). Check out your local humane society's site for more info about fostering a pet.

Create Your Own Memes

Think you have what it takes to go viral? Dream up your own funny memes and bring them to life with easy-to-use sites like *Meme Generator* and *Make a Meme*. Even if you're not interested in social media fame, you can make one with an inside joke and send it to your BFF.

Throw a Potluck Party

When everyone brings a dish, no one leaves hungry! Make it a theme party if you'd like (e.g., a Greek oasis, Hawaiian luau, or Spanish fiesta), and create a sign-up spreadsheet to make sure appetizers, main dishes, desserts, and drinks are all divided evenly among the guests.

Host a Jenga Tournament

Make this ultimate party game even more competitive by playing it tournament-style! Have some friends over, set some rules (only using one hand at a time, for example), and choose a fun prize for the Jengamaster.

Play with Paint

When's the last time you got to get your hands messy for fun? Summon up your inner child with a painting project! Make a self-portrait with pastels and a few paintbrushes, or throw it back to kindergarten and finger-paint to your creative heart's content. If you want to try some off-the-wall ideas, here are a few: Paint Bubble Wrap and use it to print designs on paper, use a paper plate to make spin art (just peek online for more info), or cut shapes in a sponge to create DIY stencils.

Get a Head Start on Holiday Decorating

The holidays will be here before you know it, and they will definitely be hectic. But it's never too early to start planning! Avoid last-minute stress by getting some of your decor ready to go now, before you have to make an expensive trip to the store. Some glittery pine cone centerpieces or handmade ornaments will get you off to a good start. You can also hand-weave a wreath from artificial flowers or vines, or build a personalized Advent calendar. Uninspired by crafts? Shop online for your decorations—if you buy out-of-season, you might score a really sweet deal.

Make Stress-Relieving Slime

In search of a hands-on stress buster? Mix up some white glue with water, Borax powder (found at most grocery stores), and the food coloring of your choice to make your own stretchy, gooey slime! When you're feeling restless, work out your tension by pulling, pinching, squeezing, and shaping your creation. For a lazy version, look up popular #slime accounts on *Instagram* that show close-up videos of hands playing with different colors and styles of slime. It's totally soothing!

Creep Yourself Out with Episodes of *The Twilight Zone*

Modern-day horror movies are terrifying, but back in the fifties and sixties, Rod Serling was creating a unique, spooky sensation in black and white: *The Twilight Zone* series. With 156 episodes, each offering a stand-alone story, you can watch all six seasons chronologically, or skip around to favorite episodes like "The Monsters Are Due on Maple Street" and "Eye of the Beholder." Think of it as the precursor to the dark social commentary in the contemporary *Netflix* series *Black Mirror*. Compare episodes of the two shows for a creepy (in a *fun* way!) night in.

Host a Book Swap

Pay the joy of a good book forward by sharing it with someone else. A book swap is a fun take on the dull, everyday library visit—plus, you get personalized recommendations from people who know you well and may have the perfect book in mind. Send an invite asking close friends to bring novels, old cookbooks, and biographies they've read and are ready to part with to a get-together with snacks and drinks. Everyone will leave armed with new books to devour—and an untouched bank account!

Collect Canned Goods

Those cans of creamed corn and green beans lurking in your pantry since you-don't-know-when could provide meals for people in need. Give back to your community by collecting a box of canned and prepackaged goods to donate to a shelter or food drive. Some of the most needed items at shelters, charities, and drives include canned tuna, peanut butter, canned fruit, nonperishable wrapped snacks like granola bars, and olive oil. To find your local food bank, you can go to FeedingAmerica.org and type in your zip code. Drop off the assortment at a local charity on your next errands run.

Treat Your Nails

Why head to a salon and dish out all that money when you can pamper your digits right at home? With just a couple of easy-to-find tools, you'll have confidence-boosting, healthy nails—and no one will be able to tell you DIYed them. (Nail polish is optional!) Here's how to give yourself a solo spa treatment with long-lasting results:

- Clean your finger or toe nails with a swipe of nail polish remover if there is any lingering polish.
- Use a nail file to smooth out rough edges in long strokes.
- Push back the cuticles and use a buffer to get the surface of the nails super clean.
- Wash your hands or feet and rub in a nice thick coat of lotion.
- If you are adding polish, wipe your nails with some more polish remover, then apply a clear base coat polish. Follow with the color of your choice, then finish with a top coat to lock in the sheen.
- While you wait for the paint to dry—give it at least thirty minutes to be really sure—catch up on your favorite podcast or indulge in a TV show.

Reread Your Favorite Book from English Class

Maybe you loved *Things Fall Apart*, or couldn't get enough of anything by George Orwell. Reading an old favorite with a fresh perspective and new life experiences in play will help you discover all kinds of new magic in a familiar story.

Knit

With just a pair of knitting needles and some yarn, you can whip up a hat, scarf, sweater…or just a bookmark. To learn, choose from dozens of easy online tutorials—and don't worry about making mistakes! With a little practice, you'll be purling like a pro in no time.

Make Dinner with Only Things You Already Have

What can you do with string cheese, romaine lettuce, chicken thighs, and Greek yogurt? Skip the grocery store and see what you can put together in your own kitchen with a random batch of ingredients. You might even discover a new favorite recipe!

Make a Bucket List

Not to be all morbid or anything, but what do you want to do before you...buy the farm? Start keeping a running list of all the countries you want to visit, activities you want to try, landmarks you want to see, adrenaline rushes you want to feel—everything you dream of doing in either the short or long term. Formally drawing up a bucket list can actually help you focus on your goals and cement your values. So get writing!

Have a French-Themed Dinner

Why dress up and shell out the big bucks for a fancy restaurant when you can bring Paris right to your kitchen table? Invite over a few of your best *amis*, or host a solo supper to treat yourself. For ambience, light some classy candles and play dreamy French music by Edith Piaf or Charlotte Gainsbourg. Start your dinner party with stinky cheeses and maybe some pâté, then whip up a batch of crepes. (You can make these easily in a large skillet!) For dessert, have a delicious apple tarte tatin or madeleines dipped in luscious chocolate. Bon appétit!

Simplify Your Life

The joy of missing out is all about finding balance between the chaotic outside world and your internal headspace. And if you've been feeling the squeeze of stress, you might have tilted too far toward those external pressures. Rebalance both realms by taking a step back and setting an intention to scale down in all areas of your life. Clearing out your belongings, your daily calendar, and your thoughts can re-energize your life and make you feel more intentional about how you move through the world. Here's how to do it:

- **Your possessions.** Material goods cost money and take up room in your home. Donate, sell, or give away anything that's hogging space or giving you anxiety.
- **Your schedule.** Train yourself to go about your day with intention. In the time you spend scrolling social media, for example, could you actually be sending an email to a faraway friend? Re-evaluate which parts of your day are the most important to you and feel the peace of skipping what's not so important. Spend some of that freed-up time doing something for yourself, like reading a good book.
- **Your mind.** Mental clutter, which often expresses itself through anxiety, makes for a tired soul. Practice spiritual minimalism by focusing on living in the present moment and clearing unwanted worries from your head. Meditation, mantras, and breathing exercises are all helpful in training your focus back to the present when you feel it straying into the past or future.

Watch *Parks and Recreation*

If you've never seen this seven-season NBC sitcom about life at an Indiana parks department, you're missing out. The show helped launch the careers of beloved actors like Aubrey Plaza, Chris Pratt, and Nick Offerman, and stars big names like Amy Poehler and Rob Lowe in hilarious, super quotable roles. But its real strength is in the dynamic, funny relationships it portrays among a diverse mix of officemates. You'll laugh at Poehler's high-energy portrayal of bureaucrat Leslie Knope, and tear up at the show's sweetest moments of love and friendship between colleagues.

Mend Your Clothes

Sure, it's not the most entertaining activity, but just think how grateful you'll be once you put on those repaired jeans or finally button up your favorite coat all the way again. If you've never done your own repairs, it's a totally easy entry into sewing! To reattach a button, all you'll need is a needle and thread in the right color. Knot the end of the thread, then loop the needle back and forth through the fabric until the button feels secure, and tie the knot off on the interior side of the clothing. Sewing a patch is as simple as stitching around the outside of the patch fabric to adhere it to your torn jeans or jacket. Still intimidated? Online tutorials make it easy to follow along and have your mending done in no time.

Do *The New York Times*'s 36 Questions

In 2015, writer Mandy Len Catron published an essay in *The New York Times* about a study that successfully used a series of specific questions to create intimacy between two people. Pick a friend or your partner, find a quiet space, and go through these questions together. Will they help you get closer to your friend, or fall even more in love with your partner?

Call Your Grandparents

Give them a ring just to let them know you love them and are thinking of them. You know they'll be thrilled!

Build Something Majestic with LEGOs

Borrow a set of LEGOs from a friend with kids and construct a grand castle, serene village, stately bridge—or whatever your heart (and hands) desire. When you're finished, you can leave your masterpiece up or tear it down and build something new.

Cook the Perfect Omelet

Did you know that omelets can actually be one of the most intricate things to cook? But if you can make scrambled eggs, you can also create this light and fluffy breakfast treat that also makes a filling lunch or dinner. Hit up your favorite recipe book or site and master this eggy delicacy, whether you choose the French version (eggs only) or the American style (eggs plus vegetables, meat, or other yummy add-ins). Plus, it only takes about five minutes to cook; so if at first you don't succeed, repeated tries are definitely doable! Serve with a side of home-fried potatoes if you'd like.

Set a Goal

Choosing an intention for the future can help you better balance your time. By naming and writing down your goal, you visualize its fulfillment and put strong energy out into the universe. It can be a small one for the day, like finally taking that package to the post office, or a grander one for the month or even year, like developing and sticking to a fitness plan. To maximize your chance of achieving your goal, try setting one that's SMART (Specific, Measurable, Attainable, Relevant, and Time-bound). For example, deciding to "apply for six new jobs by March 1" is more specific, measurable, attainable, relevant, and time-bound than "change career."

Write a Letter to an Inmate

If you are looking to make a difference (and enjoy some time at home) you can find a prison pen pal through WriteAPrisoner.com. The site lets you search for interested participants at different correctional facilities and connect with them via snail mail or a secure email address. Studies show that inmates who maintain social contact with the outside world foster a healthier emotional state of being and are less likely to experience recidivism (the tendency of an offender to reoffend once released). Locate someone whose profile resonates with you and reach out to start making a positive difference today.

Watch a Movie from Before You Were Born

Everyone has their favorite films from their youth, but it can be just as enjoyable to go back even further and check out some classics from before your time. Peek into a door from the past with a film from at least a decade before you were born. Try a Charlton Heston epic from the fifties, a sixties war drama, or a seventies horror flick. Bonus activity: Watch one of your parents' favorite films and discuss it with them afterward.

Own Your "Flaws"

Shame about revealing your true self can stop you from doing so, so much. Deep down, you may believe that there are parts of your personality that you need to conceal before others fully like you. Sound familiar? If you've self-sabotaged a budding relationship or blamed yourself for something that was actually out of your control, you might be letting shame dictate your own worth. It's time to let go of these harmful hang-ups by embracing who you are— every aspect of your own beautiful soul.

Practice looking at things you might think of as flaws—like moodiness, or impatience, or a complete lack of willpower in the face of a plate of tempting French fries—as positive or at least neutral aspects that help make up the wonderful you. List out each "flaw," and go through them one by one, asking, "How might this help me in some situations?" If you can't think of benefits, explore the ways it might be neutral. For example, eating those fries one day doesn't cancel out healthy choices you can make the next. (Also keep in mind that these things differ from those habits you can work on improving to become your best self. These perceived deficiencies are actually the quirky things about you that make you wonderfully unique.) Over time, you can learn to stop letting shame preclude you from the vibrant life you deserve.

Register to Vote

Voting is one of the most fundamental rights you have as a citizen of a democracy. It takes only a few minutes and puts the power of change in your hands. After all, elections don't only settle who wins which political race; they also allocate funding for schools, hospitals, and other public institutions, and pass laws that affect you and the other people in your community. If you don't vote for what matters to you, who will? If you have already registered, get a leg up on your next chance to exercise that right by researching your area's next election candidates and their positions on different issues.

Learn to Trim Your Own Hair

Home might not be the best place to make a *drastic* hair change. (Unless you're a professional stylist, in which case, buzz away!) But with just a little finesse and the right pair of scissors, you can easily trim your own locks and put off going to the salon for a little bit longer. Some of the easiest trims to make at home are on bangs and split ends. A good trim will make your hair look and feel more vibrant! Remember to always cut your hair while it's damp, use really sharp shears designed for hair cutting, and focus on only trimming away strays and splitting ends.

Tour a Foreign Country on *Google Earth*

Pass on the pricey flight and use your computer to transport your-self to a stunning place thousands of miles away. With just a few clicks, you can scope out the Eiffel Tower, chill on Bondi Beach in Australia, make a virtual pilgrimage to Mecca, or explore the Atlantic Ocean without ever having to shuffle through an airport.

Cook Indian Food

It's actually really easy to make samosas, palak paneer, dal, and more of your spicy, savory favorites right in the comfort of your own kitchen. Take a pass on the takeout this time, and whip up a South Asian feast at home!

Research the History of Where You Live

Do you know when your town was founded? Or when your state became a state? When was your neighborhood built? Spend some time getting to know your home city, state, or country and emerge with a new appreciation for the geography and culture around you.

Revitalize Your Coffee Maker

While you get energized from each pot of your homemade java, your coffee maker gets a little slower and gunkier. Dirty coffee makers also make the perfect breeding ground for mold and yeast and other things you don't want, so be sure to clean yours out regularly. Run white vinegar diluted with water through your coffee maker for two cycles, then flush it out by running two more cycles of just plain water. Make sure to also wash each removable part in the dishwasher or with hot water and soap in your sink. Your next pot of coffee will taste so much fresher!

Rewatch Your All-Time Favorite Movie

Everyone has that movie that they somehow never tire of watching. Is yours *The Shining*? *When Harry Met Sally*? *The Hangover*? Watching your favorite film—the one you can quote every line from and perfectly describe scenes from—can be a huge source of comfort, just like cozying up on your worn-in sofa. Lean into the warm hug of familiarity by watching a cherished flick for the 7,684th time. Who knows? You might notice something this time around that you've missed all these years. Or you might just enjoy the feeling of reuniting with an old "friend."

DIY a Spa Night

Whether you want to make this a fun event with a friend or two, or just relax solo, gather up some lemons and lavender and get your fill of zen body scrubs. There are tons of recipes online that you can make with ingredients you already have in your house! In between spa treatments, keep the serenity going by sipping on healthy fruit juices or tea, and be sure to light a candle or turn on an essential oil diffuser for a relaxing aroma. Don't forget the cucumber slices for your eyes!

Listen to a Vinyl Record

Streaming music online is convenient, sure, but nothing beats the old-school sound and character of the classic LP. And the great thing about listening to music the old-fashioned way is that you can find tons of used equipment online cheap or even for free. Give your streaming music library a day off, score a record player, and pick out some used albums (the Rolling Stones, Bob Dylan, and Jimi Hendrix are all good places to start). You'll be spinning in no time. Plus, watching a record gently turn is surprisingly soothing.

Restore Your Old Furniture

Instead of getting rid of that worn-out armchair, reupholster it! A dingy bookcase can be rejuvenated with a fresh coat of bright paint. With a few simple techniques found online, you can make your old pieces new again *and* save money and time by skipping the store.

Play *The Oregon Trail*

Yes, the same fun game from grade school! Remember how exciting it was to reach the Willamette Valley? You can still go hunting and ford the river in the modern Internet version of your favorite computer class time-waster.

Buy Birthday Gifts

Avoid the last-minute scramble by snagging presents online for your besties ahead of time so they're ready to be wrapped and gifted when the big day comes. You'll never send something belated again! Plus, it gives you more time to find a bargain.

Master the Moonwalk

Michael Jackson made it look impossible, but you can actually learn to do the dance he made so popular by following along to an online tutorial. Put on some socks, find a polished floor, and get ready to feel a little foolish for a bit (hey, moonwalking doesn't come naturally to most) while having a great time. The dance move itself involves a simple repetition of weight shifting and foot gliding, so it gets easier the more you practice. Try filming yourself on your smartphone or practicing in front of a mirror until you have it down; you just might have a new move to show off at weddings when you're done.

Throw a Tiki Party

Tiki bars are loud and crowded, but when you host your own tropical fete at home, you are in charge of the guest list and the vibe. You can also customize anything you want, from serving only nonalcoholic drinks to using dry ice to make an extra-special effect in the punch bowl. Make sure you have plenty of snacks on hand, whether you go with traditional island fare like shrimp egg rolls or your own twist on a tiki menu. Then whip up a big bowl of rum punch, put out leis and themed glassware, and turn on some beachy tunes. Hawaiian shirts optional!

Turn Your Bedroom Into a Sanctuary

You spend at least one-third of your life in your bedroom, so having a cozy, inviting, and relaxing space will not only help you sleep, but create a safe area for solitude and that much-needed time to recharge your batteries. Try these methods for making your bedroom homey and sacred:

- **Have lots of blankets.** What's cozier than snuggling under a ton of blankets? Knit your own or order your favorite soft quilts online.
- **Purchase a speaker or white noise machine for muting irritating sounds.** Drown out the sounds of actual traffic outside your place, or mental traffic in your mind, by playing some soft music or gentle, calming tones.
- **Accent with cozy rugs.** Make sure you never have to put your feet down on cold wood or tile in the mornings again. For maximum softness, look for faux-fur or shag rugs.
- **Splurge on a memory foam or pillow-top mattress cover.** Even if your current mattress isn't ideal, you can give it a premium upgrade by trading in your current mattress pad for an extra-soft topper that puts you right to sleep.
- **Banish overhead lighting.** Ceiling lights make everything look harsh. Score some tableside lamps or string lights that give off a gentle glow, or use a Himalayan salt lamp to create a soothing pink aura.

Clean Out Your Fridge

As an ancient guru once said, "Clean fridge, clean mind." Okay, maybe no legitimate sage ever uttered these words, but every kitchen can definitely benefit from a good refrigerator deep-clean. To begin, get rid of any produce or other products that are past their expiration date, and nix leftovers or condiments that have overstayed their welcome. Next, wipe down the insides of your fridge with all-purpose cleaner, getting rid of all those unidentifiable stains, spills, crumbs, and odors. Be sure to clean the produce bins and the exterior door and handles as well. A spotless fridge will make you smile every time you crack it open to root around for a snack or embark on a new cooking adventure.

Laugh Until Your Sides Ache

Did you know that laughing has actual health benefits? Whether you're cracking up from watching a funny TV show or hosting friends who have known you forever, laughing can boost your immune system, ease pain symptoms, and improve your mood. Laughing is also an instant stress reliever. Plus, there's nothing like that joyous feeling of really connecting over a deep belly laugh. Find your favorite funny experience—be it your favorite humor writer's column or that friend who has all the best jokes—and have a long, healthy giggle fit.

Strengthen Your Brain with Mental Puzzles

Logic games and brain teasers aren't just for fun. Studies show that doing some type of mental challenge regularly can boost your memory, invigorate your overall brain activity, and keep your wits sharp to stave off mental decline as you get older. They're also a great alternative to staring mindlessly at a TV or phone screen. Grab a book of logic or number problems, or print off a free PDF of brain teasers, and get cracking!

Watch *Spirited Away*

Every genre of film has its own classics. For adventure, it might include the Indiana Jones series, and for romantic comedies, *Clueless* and *Annie Hall*. One of the most iconic films in the anime genre is surely the 2001 Japanese movie *Spirited Away*, which follows ten-year-old Chihiro as she gets caught up in a fantastical adventure. Hayao Miyazaki, one of the greatest anime filmmakers of all time, creates a visually stunning landscape of complex characters (set to an award-winning soundtrack) that make this movie feel like a universe within itself. *Spirited* is a great intro to the anime genre if you're new around these parts.

Send a Postcard from Your City

Head to the touristy part of town, score a souvenir postcard, and brighten someone's day with a simple, funny message!

Make Refreshing Fruit-Infused Water

Tap water and a large helping of delicious fruit can create a rejuvenating thirst quencher. Try creative combinations like blackberry and cucumber.

Do Sit-Ups

Strengthening your core not only helps you build that six-pack you've dreamed of; it can also help your posture, boost your flexibility, and make you stronger for other workouts. Plus, you can do sit-ups anytime, anywhere, with no equipment or gym membership. (Crunches count!)

Host a Horror Movie Night

Instead of going out into the world—which can be a little scary itself!—have friends over for a little at-home suspense. Here's what you need to throw a spooky movie marathon for your besties:

- **A killer lineup.** Pick a theme like "Old School" (*The Amityville Horror, The Exorcist,* and classic Hitchcock films), "Zombies" (*28 Days Later, Dawn of the Dead, Resident Evil*), or "Thriller" (*Get Out, Misery, Silence of the Lambs*). Your marathon could also center around international picks, camping/the woods (*The Blair Witch Project,* anyone?), or Halloween.
- **Spooky icebreakers.** Get the party started with some paranormal small-talk. Who believes in ghosts? What's the scariest thing they've ever witnessed? How would they survive a zombie attack?
- **Skin-tingling snacks.** You're gonna need some comfort food to come down from the adrenaline rush. Think macaroni and cheese, cupcakes, and blood-red punch.
- **Lots of pillows and blankets.** These will be good for chilly moments, but also for hiding your eyes behind when the action gets super intense.
- **Games to take the edge off.** When you need a break from the scaries, have a quick game ready to get everyone laughing, like Cards Against Humanity or What Do You Meme?

Watch a Documentary

Vegging out on the couch never gets old, but you can take your next relaxation session to the next level by also learning something new with an interesting documentary. Documentaries are a great way to stimulate your brain and also give you something new to talk about with friends, family members, or a significant other. You can explore different countries and ways of living, or dig deeper into history, politics, or a topic of your choice that you're already pretty well versed in. Documentaries have their own category on most online video streaming services, so it's a snap to find one that suits your interests.

Learn How to Play the Ukulele

If piano lessons never really tickled *your* ivories, or you got bored with the classic violin, there's still an instrument that could be the perfect fit for you: the humble ukulele! You couldn't ask for a simpler instrument; the ukulele comes with only four strings and is a breeze to strum a fun rhythm on. But don't let its simplicity belie its ability to create great music. In fact, the ukulele can transform traditional songs into lilting, island-ready jams. Look up an easy how-to video and some sheet music, and borrow a ukulele from a musical friend (or find a cheap option online), and before you know it you'll be making up your own tunes and singing along.

Shop for Furniture

Furniture can be so expensive! Not to mention the overeager sales staff checking in every other minute when you just want the chance to look at different couch models for yourself. The best place to scour for bargains is from the comfort of your own easy chair—and sweatpants—where you can track down some great pieces without having to run around town. Hunt for treasures on discount sites like *Overstock* and *Wayfair*, and browse the clearance section on *West Elm*. Even if you can't afford that killer new settee yet, sometimes just adding it to your virtual shopping cart scratches that "gotta have this now" itch.

Get Rid of What's Bothering You

Sometimes simple, tangible things can have a real impact on your mental health. Visualize yourself letting go of each grievance you are feeling as they flow from your mind, through a pen, and onto a piece of paper in front of you. Your list—or longer paragraph—of what's bothering you can include everything from the big (a work crisis) to the small (running out of almond milk for your cereal today). Once you are done writing, crumple up the paper, then tear it into tiny pieces and get rid of it by either throwing it in a trash can or burning it safely over a controlled flame. Go about your day with renewed positivity!

Play a Round of Twister

All you need is the mat and spinner and a group of friends to have a blast! If you haven't owned this classic party game since you were in grade school, you can always DIY it with circles of brightly colored paper and a spinner fashioned from cardboard.

Draw a Chalk Masterpiece on the Asphalt

Grab some funky-colored sidewalk chalk and use your driveway or the walkway in front of your home as your very own canvas. There's something liberating about creating art that will only last until the next rainfall.

Teach Yourself to Code

With some simple coding skills, you can build your own website, make an app, or just gain deeper insight into what goes into the Internet and the devices you use every day. Purchase a book online, check out how-to videos, or take an online class from *Udemy* or *Codecademy*.

Bake Your Own Bread

In the time you'd spend at one energy-sucking cocktail party, you can produce a delicious loaf of homemade rye bread! Warning: Once you've tasted a thick slice of homemade toasted bread, you'll never want to buy it from the store again. And while bread recipes have a reputation for being finicky, it all depends on the specific ingredients and process. Below, you'll find a quick overview of great homemade options:

- **Naan.** A good starter bread is a flatbread like naan, which doesn't require much rising or kneading and can be cooked on a stovetop instead of in an oven. You can add herbs and garlic at the end for a big kick of flavor.
- **Soft pretzels.** These will require a baking soda bath and some solid wrist work to make a twisty pretzel shape. (But the dough also tastes delicious as mini-loaves.)
- **Sandwich bread.** For a hearty bread that's not too fussy, bake a couple loaves of white or whole-wheat sandwich bread that you can slice for sandwiches or toast. You'll want to make sure you have at least four hours to spare for rising the dough before baking.
- **Sourdough.** To make sourdough, you'll need to make or purchase a sourdough starter. You can create your own by combining flour and water in a bowl and refrigerating it for several days, "feeding" it each day by adding more flour and water. For a shortcut, borrow some starter from a friend, or have it delivered from your local bakery or bread shop.

Watch a Movie with Subtitles

Subtitles are often labeled a distracting nuisance, but you're missing out on some of the world's best films when you only watch movies made in English! Trade in your habit of browsing solely American movies by giving international films a chance. Great places to start are the German film *Run Lola Run*, Brazil's *Cidade de Deus*, and the Italian classic *La Vita è Bella*. The extra step of reading captions will challenge your brain in a good way, and you will expand your cinematic horizons beyond the realm of English-language-only movies.

Curb Stress

Feeling on edge? You can channel some of that nervous energy into fiddling with an anxiety-relieving tool like a stress ball or fidget spinner. Fidget spinners surged in popularity among middle and high school students recently, but they're not just for kids. Hands-on devices can provide a great physical outlet for excess energy, and also take your mind off a churning sea of worries. Purchase a spinner or a stress ball online, and give it a try while you're listening to a podcast, watching TV, or trying to fight Sunday-night pre-workweek dread.

Throw a Clothes Swap Party

The biggest downside to shopping for new clothes is the whole going to the mall part. (And that's to say nothing of the terrible fitting rooms that always manage to make you feel bad.) Do a good deed by letting everyone skip the crowded shopping spree—do it at your house instead! Ask your friends to go through their closets and bring the spoils over: shoes, dresses, shirts, or bottoms they've outgrown or never wear, and jewelry they're tired of. Serve wine or lemonade, have everyone pick a random number, and take turns choosing among items. Presto: Everyone gets a bunch of new clothes for their wardrobe—for free! (You might want to set some haggling rules so no one gets too cutthroat.)

Make Homemade Popsicles

What to do when you're craving a cold treat, but the only thing in your freezer is a leftover bag of frozen peas? Skip the grocery store and blend up your own tasty fruit-sicles right in your kitchen. You control the flavors, so if you love watermelon but hate grape, enjoy tasty watermelon popsicles for days! If you're feeling fancy, you can experiment with adding yogurt or cold brew coffee, and if you don't have ice pop molds, you can always use small cups (Dixie cups work really well). Good luck stopping after just one.

Design a De-Stressing Playlist

When you need to tune out the world, tune in to a custom playlist of all the music that makes you relax—or grin from ear to ear. Crank it when you're feeling tired or blue, and let some good old-fashioned music therapy wash your stress away.

Draw Portraits with a Friend

Whether your artistic abilities clock in at stick figures or professional sketches, you'll still have fun trying to capture the likeness of a close friend or partner on paper. And while you work, have them draw a picture of you too; then compare results at the end and crown a drawing master.

Read *Letters to a Young Poet* by Rainer Maria Rilke

From 1902 to 1908, Rilke, then an established Austrian poet, wrote ten letters to a young man and aspiring poet who'd reached out to him for life advice before entering the German military. Important themes that Rilke stressed, like cultivating a rich inner life and resisting the harsh words of critics, still ring true today. Plus, the work is now in the public domain, so you can read it online for free.

Relax with Gregorian Chants

Named after Pope Gregory I, Gregorian liturgical chants were designed to accompany Catholic mass back in the ninth century. Even if you're not religious, you will find the gentle rise and fall of the meter of these chants soothing. The fact that they're sung in Latin also means you won't get distracted by the lyrics (unless you're fluent in Latin, that is!), making them a good choice for background music when studying or working.

Get Some Sun

Anyone who's had to live through a week or more of nonstop cloudy or rainy weather knows the uplifting benefits that sunlight can have on your mood. Getting some natural sunlight boosts your levels of vitamin D (the nutrient linked to emotional wellness) and triggers the release of serotonin and other feel-good nervous system chemicals. To reap these rewards, you don't have to go sun-tanning for hours—which can actually be dangerous for your skin. Instead, sit in a sun-filled area of your house, or take a short walk around your property on a sunny day. If you're going to be out for longer than ten to twenty minutes, make sure to apply sunscreen.

Make a Flower Crown

If you've been to a rustic wedding or just seen social media posts from friends at music festivals, you probably know that flower circlets have been—and honestly always will be—all the rage. But you don't need pricey Coachella tickets to get your bohemian vibe on; once you've learned what a cinch it is to DIY your own flower crown, you'll be shocked that people spend so much money on designer ones (Dolce & Gabbana marketed one at over $1,400!). To weave your own, you only need a few simple things:

- Floral wire
- Floral tape
- Wire cutters
- Flowers of your choice (real or fake!)

First, form the wire into a circle that loosely fits on the crown of your head. Next, carefully cut short pieces of your flowers and tape them by the stems to the circle to form a leafy base. If you have both greenery and blooms, first tape the greenery to the wire to form a base, then add the flowers. That's it! You've got a lovely crown that's perfect for your next outdoor concert...or for wearing with pride while you flit around the house.

Watch Cute Goat Videos

Have you seen jumping goats? "Talking" goats? *Fainting* goats? When you're feeling blue, cue up some stress-relieving goat videos and laugh your tension away. (Don't worry, no goats are harmed in the making of these!)

Chew Gum

Research shows chomping on sugar-free gum can reduce stress, ease digestion and acid reflux, prevent cavities, and even improve your memory. Time to *chew*-se your favorite flavor and start reaping the benefits.

Teach Yourself a Line Dance

Even the most ungraceful among us can learn a simple line dance like the Cha-Cha Slide, Electric Slide, or Cupid Shuffle. Rock your new moves at your next wedding, bar or bat mitzvah, or country-western affair!

Create a Zine

Zines, short print magazines designed for viral reading pleasure, allow you to create an eye-catching collection full of your thoughts, sketches, or whatever you want to tell the world. Pick a topic for your zine and start to work on your words and/or drawings. You can also find tons of ideas and helpful tips online for creating a great zine. And if you want to involve other voices, put out a call for writers to contribute. When you're done, you can mail your zine to subscribers, sell them at a local bookstore, or give them away at a favorite coffee shop.

Try Qigong

Qigong (pronounced "chee-gong") is a Chinese spiritual practice that combines slow, flowing body motions with mental focus and meditation. Qigong takes both physical and mental concentration, and encourages you to find and zero in on your mind-body connection. You can practice it while standing up (one form of standing qigong is tai chi), sitting, or even lying down. Whether you have four minutes or forty, you can benefit from learning a gentle, purposeful art that you can practice anywhere—especially in your own home.

DIY Burrito Bowls

Getting dressed and going out for Tex-Mex? That's hard. Having a burrito party in your own kitchen? That's more like it. Whether you're feeding an entire family or just yourself, a crowd-pleasing burrito bowl bar (say that ten times fast!) is not only an inexpensive option, but also lets everyone customize their dinner however they'd like. Just set out the following ingredients, give everyone a bowl, and let them construct away:

- A batch of cooking rice, white or brown
- Black or pinto beans
- Fajita veggies such as corn
- Tomatoes
- Cooked meat of your choice
- Pico de gallo
- Guacamole or chopped avocado
- Lettuce shreds
- Hot sauce
- Sour cream
- Chopped cilantro
- Shredded cheese

To accompany your burrito bowls, make a big batch of limeade or margaritas and set out a bowl of chips for snacking and dipping. For dessert, whip up some churros or flan.

Rearrange Your Furniture

Make your home feel new again without buying a thing by switching up the pieces you already have. By changing the flow of a room or letting different furniture take center stage, you'll reinvigorate the look and feel of your favorite spaces. Try putting your couch at a different angle or moving your easy chair to face the window. Switching a wall mirror to a different wall or moving furniture pieces ever so slightly away from the walls can make any room feel larger and airier. Even just changing up the view from your bed can reinvent the vibe of your entire space and bedtime.

Make a Challenging Recipe

Does the thought of making a soufflé scare you? Do lamb recipes leave you feeling panicked in the grocery store aisle? The idea of trying to concoct your own croissants or lobster thermidor might be enough to make you want to throw in the towel and hit up a restaurant, but don't fear! There are dozens of easy-to-follow videos online—plus, it's okay to not get things perfectly in your first try. So think beyond your normal spaghetti or roasted chicken routine and take a walk on the adventurous side for your next meal. Pick a cuisine you order often when you go out to eat, and walk through it step by step. The payoff may be more delicious than the restaurant version.

Teach Yourself a Computer Program

Think how grateful you'll be when you can use your new skills in Photoshop, QuickBooks, or Salesforce at work or a new job *without* having to consult a beginner's guide in front of your boss.

Stir Up a Soothing Golden Latte

Turmeric gives this warm drink its gorgeous golden hue. Combine the nondairy milk of your choice with ground turmeric, pure honey, ground cinnamon, and a dash of ground black pepper. It's caffeine-free, so you can drink it before bed to get ready for a long, rejuvenating night's sleep.

Watch *Twin Peaks*

This nineties crime drama series set in the fictional town of Twin Peaks, Washington, had only two seasons, but it quickly gained a cult following and was revived in 2017 for a much-anticipated third season. Settle back with a "damn fine cup of coffee" and immerse yourself in the mystery of who killed Laura Palmer.

Sleep In

As much as getting out of bed early can make for a great, produc-
tive day, sometimes you just need a good ol' fashioned lie-in on a
day off to recharge. Plus, studies show that getting fewer than six
hours of solid bed rest per night can contribute to long-term health
issues in the future, like hypertension, depression, diabetes, and
memory loss. Let everyone else hit the farmers' market and running
trails early this weekend, because you have some important and
healthy R&R ahead of you. Turn off your alarm, snuggle in, and let
your body wake up whenever it feels natural. Come the next work-
day you'll get back into your normal wake-up schedule feeling well-
rested and rejuvenated.

Do a Super Hard Jigsaw Puzzle

Roll up your sleeves, turn off your phone, and clear off your coffee
table: It's puzzle time. It's going to involve some serious homebody
hours, because you won't be tempted to leave the house when you
have a 5,000-piece challenge in front of you! An old-fashioned jig-
saw puzzle doesn't require any screen time and can be its own form
of meditation as you focus solely on the work you're doing bit-by-
bit to restore a picture to its complete glory. Really feel the weight
of each puzzle piece as you snap it into place. When you're done,
preserve your masterpiece with a puzzle glue that lets you frame it,
or simply take it apart and put it all back in the box for a future day
inside.

Host an English Tea

Want to have a get-together that has less of a "party hard" vibe? Enjoy a classy afternoon by setting up a traditional tea party for your friends (or yourself). For the star beverage, brew up a big pot of Earl Grey or PG Tips and make sure there is plenty of milk on hand. Snacks-wise, pick your delicious English poison: Crumpets, scones, petit fours, tartlets, and crustless sandwiches will all be a hit. Keep the atmosphere non-stuffy with some corgi-themed decor (the queen's favorite dog!) and relaxing tunes. For next-level tea-time, have your guests BYOT—that's "Bring Your Own Teacup"—or ask them to wear fancy hats. *Cheerio!*

Swap Life Stories

No matter how close you are with a friend, you'll see in a whole new light once you know all about their childhood dreams, most embarrassing moments, first job, first kiss, greatest fears, and more. Here are some great questions to ask to get the ball rolling on your in-depth conversation:

- What movie did you watch on repeat when you were a kid?
- What accomplishment are you most proud of?
- How do you deal on a sad day?
- If you could live in any city in the world, where would it be?
- When was the last time you cried?
- Who's a person you miss having in your life?
- What would you tell childhood you if you could go back in time?
- What's on your bucket list?

Dive Into *The Sopranos*

The ultimate binge-worthy serial drama, *The Sopranos* tracks mob boss Tony Soprano as he tries to find, well, work-life balance between being a mafia honcho and patriarch of his family. HBO's masterpiece has been deemed one of the best TV shows of all time, and you have six seasons to keep you engrossed in the dark world of the New Jersey mob for the day or weekend.

Make S'mores

Campfires can be so overrated. The bugs, small talk, physical work—when all you wanted was some gooey dessert. You don't need to go outside to enjoy this chocolaty, marshmallowy treat! Just grab some graham crackers, marshmallows, and the chocolate bar of your choice and use your gas stove or a burning candle to create your s'mores. If you don't have a gas stove or candle, you can also bake s'mores in your oven; just arrange them open-faced on a cookie sheet and bake at 400°F for three to five minutes. It's all of the camping junk-food fun, without the outside part.

Create a Work-Life Balance

Unless you win the lottery (fingers crossed), you'll probably spend a certain amount of time each week either at a job or working from home. But just because you have to work to live doesn't mean you have to live to work. Here are a few easy ways to keep your work at work, so you can fully enjoy your personal time:

- **Set firm boundaries for time off-the-clock.** Just because it's easy to answer emails at all hours of the night doesn't mean you have to (or should). Block out the times and days when you're unavailable, and resist feeling guilty about being off the grid. You'll hopefully inspire others to see that it's not selfish or irresponsible to keep communications within certain time frames.
- **Keep your not-working time sacred.** If it's a Tuesday night and you had plans to go see a play but feel totally drained, go ahead and bow out to recharge at home. Let your nights off be fully yours to spend however you'd like, and cancel plans if they don't serve you.
- **Realign with your values.** What would you spend your time and energy on if you didn't have to worry about work? Make a list of everything you wish you had more time for and keep it nearby. Knowing what is important to you outside of the office will help you focus on how you can keep to these values and wants, and what in your life is currently in need of a little extra TLC.

Make a Dinner with Food That's the Same Color

Want a colorful, delicious challenge? Pretend you're on your favorite television cooking competition and prepare a meal with grub that's all one shade! Maybe purple potatoes as a side, eggplant Parmesan for the main event, and a fig tart for dessert, or a kale salad appetizer, pesto chicken entree, and mint chocolate cheesecake treat. (Bonus points if you pair an aptly hued beverage with your meal.) For extra competition, face off against a friend to see who can nail this color culinary challenge the best. And if you're tempted to post the result pics on social media, go for it—or just savor the art (and taste) of a job well done.

Master the Art of Folding a Fitted Bedsheet

It's. So. Hard. But if you're tired of just crumpling your fitted sheets into balls and slinging them on the shelf in your linen closet, there are tricks you can look up online that will have you folding like a pro in no time. Share your new knowledge with your partner so they can take their turn conquering the bedsheets—or teach a roommate. And if you want to take things to the next level, you can find all kinds of technical moves to master the art of folding everything in your closet, from tees and hoodies, to tablecloths and cloth napkins.

Build a Gingerbread House

You don't have to wait until the holidays to construct a sweet structure that's fun to both design *and* eat. (To make it seasonally appropriate, you can even make a gingerbread beach house or rustic cabin.) Simply follow an easy gingerbread cookie recipe to make the dough, cut it into your shapes (large squares for the walls, plus a person, trees, cobblestones for a walkway, window frames—whatever you want for your masterpiece), and bake away. Use royal icing to build the house and secure all of your elements. Finally, decorate it with candy and frosting!

Read *You Are a Badass* by Jen Sincero

Sincero has written an inspiring, insightful guide for all of the people who are put off by traditional self-help books. With wit and a no-nonsense attitude, she encourages you to hurdle over your fears and move forward into a purposeful future.

Infuse Your Booze

Vanilla bean vodka? Earl Grey gin? Add a little more flavor to the spirit of your choice by letting fruit or herbs steep in it in a sealed bottle for a few days. Cheers!

Start a Cactus Garden

"Regular" plants add tons of leafy pleasure to your digs, but they also require a certain degree of maintenance and sunlight. Enter the simple, low-maintenance cactus. Not only do cacti look cool (and come in a variety of styles), but they're also super easy to grow and nurture. Many types of cacti bloom, lending a burst of easy-to-care-for flowers to your space. For an indoor version of a cactus garden, build a terrarium and stock it with miniature cacti plants, being sure to put it in indirect sunlight, and water it only once every few weeks. If you have the room and right climate outside (they love mild winters), experiment with cactus landscaping.

Make Your Own Bagels

You won't have to leave the house in the morning for a warm bagel with cream cheese when you bake up a big batch of your own. Making bagels is a multistep process that involves letting a dough rise, shaping it into bagel rings, boiling them, and then baking them. But don't let that freak you out! It's actually simple to do through a video tutorial or easy-to-follow instructions online. Plus, it's the perfect excuse to spend a whole day inside! ("I'd love to, but my bagels are rising.") And the homemade reward is way more delicious than any store-bought bagel ever could be.

Cue Up an Audiobook

Listening to a good book can be even more soothing than reading one, so give an audiobook service like Audible a try. You might be surprised by how easily you can still get lost in a story, even if you aren't physically turning the pages.

Score a Bargain

Scoring a 50 percent discount from the comfort of your couch somehow feels more satisfying than finding 70 percent off an item after hours of traipsing through the mall. Use the power of the Internet to help you hunt down the best sales on sites like *Groupon* and *Craigslist*, and rest easy while your finds get delivered to you.

Tie-Dye a T-Shirt

All you need are some dyes (you can find tons of colors online, as well as full tie-dye kits) and a few rubber bands to turn a boring white tee into psychedelic streetwear. Spend an afternoon making a tee that's just as funky as you are! If you have extras, you can give them away as gifts.

Bubble Up Some Fizzy Water

Use a machine like the handy SodaStream to infuse boring old tap water with bubbly CO_2 and make hydrating that much more effervescent. You'll save money on all those cans of seltzer you've been buying, and help save the planet too. Plus, you can experiment with different flavored syrups if you're more of a soda person. For a real DIY experiment, try adding some fresh muddled fruit or hand-squeezed fruit juices to your bubbles for a full-flavor mocktail.

Leave a Nice Voicemail Message

When's the last time you actually left or received a personal voicemail? Still thinking? Phone messages can feel like a dying art these days, so why not revive it with one that your friend or family member will be excited to play? Call a loved one when you know they're offline or their phone is on silent and leave a sweet greeting to make their day. One idea: Do a countdown of five things you really, really love about that person. They may even save the message to listen to whenever they need a pick-me-up.

Get Dolled Up

Who ever said being all dressed up and nowhere to go was a bad thing? Indulge in some self-pampering by getting ready for a night on the town—without having to actually go outside. Put on your favorite outfit, even if it's a ball gown or a tux, style your hair, put on makeup if that's your thing, and just chill out knowing you look totally, 100 percent fabulous.

Read a Religious Text

You can find the Bible, the Talmud, the Koran, the Upanishads, the Buddhist Suttas, and more online for free. Delve into a sacred book from your tradition, or explore different spiritual beliefs.

Learn How to Say "I Love You" in Different Languages

Te amo! Je t'aime! Ich liebe Dich! See how many different languages you can memorize the world's sweetest phrase in. You can even make one of them your secret way to say "I love you" to your partner.

Give Compliments

Compliments are one of the best free gifts you can give to someone. Genuine words of praise not only make a person's day or week
or even month, but they can also reinforce your relationship with
them and encourage more honesty and gratitude. Take some time
to ruminate on what makes your friend or partner the greatest, be
it their awesome fashion sense, generous heart, or dedication to
their career or family. Get every compliment down on either paper
or your computer screen, then give them the list next time you see
them, or read it to them over the phone if they live far away.

Savor Every Delicious Bite

When you sit down to dinner or grab your next snack, practice
more mindful eating by taking the time to really enjoy your food.
The experience will be so much better, plus eating slowly and delib-
erately is actually one of the better things you can do to change
bad food habits like overeating. Your stomach takes about fifteen
minutes to realize that you're consuming food, which also means
that it is full much sooner than you realize. Eating a little slower
gives your body a chance to signal to the brain that it's all set. It can
also lead to easier digestion, increased hydration, and higher satis-
faction with your food—even if it's just an apple.

Listen to The Beatles

The full Beatles catalog is available for free on most streaming services, so take full advantage by working your way through this beloved band's entire library. Take your time exploring each record as its own work of art (that you can dance and sing along to). Along the way, savor John Lennon and Paul McCartney's catchy song-writing and unique style that somehow still sounds modern today. See if you can spot the turning point from early Beatles (more of a catchy, pop rock sound) to late Beatles (more psychedelic and eccentric).

Host a BBQ

Whether it's July...or January, you can fire up some barbecue magic and bring people together over tasty meat and seared veggies. If the weather permits, heat up your grill and invite your besties over for some old-fashioned burgers and hot dogs. If it's chilly out, bring your BBQ indoors and use a grill pan for a stovetop version. Prefer a more subdued fest? Make it a casual dinner for you and/or your partner. And don't forget the sides—they can totally make the party! Stock plenty of baked beans, potato salad, coleslaw, corn bread, pickle relish, ketchup, and yellow mustard. Bonus points for wearing an apron with a funny saying on it.

Finally Tackle That Cleaning Project

I know: *ick*. But think how great you'll feel when you look at those dust-free baseboards, shiny bathtub, or clean ceiling fans. Some ideas for where to start if you don't have a project in mind already:

- **Your cell phone.** Wipe it down with a hand sanitizer wipe or a cloth lightly spritzed with rubbing alcohol.
- **The dishwasher.** Put a cup of vinegar in the top rack and run a wash cycle to disinfect your machine.
- **The shower curtain.** You can probably put it right in the washing machine!
- **Light switches.** Clean the fingerprints off of these with a sanitary wipe.
- **Air-conditioning and heating vents.** Use a knife and a washcloth to really get in there.
- **Houseplants.** Wipe down their dusty leaves with a clean cloth.
- **Your toothbrush.** A long soak in some white vinegar will disinfect it.
- **Remote controls.** These get so grubby! Get them clean with an antibacterial wipe or alcohol-soaked cotton swab.
- **The trash can.** This is one of the most germ-filled places in your house, so clean it with all-purpose spray on the reg.
- **Reusable grocery bags.** Toss these in a laundry cycle to get them sparkling clean.
- **Earbuds.** Use a cotton swab dipped in alcohol to clean them off.
- **Ice cube trays.** A vinegar soak will help get that weird smell out.
- **Your car's steering wheel.** Use leather or all-purpose cleaner, depending on the steering wheel's material.

Bake a Batch of Cupcakes

What's better than one cake? Lots of mini cakes! Cupcakes are not only fun to eat; they're also easy to bake (even without a store-bought mix) and are the perfect vehicle for sugary, delicious frosting. Your dessert feast is as simple as throwing together some batter via an easy recipe from the Internet, pouring it into a cupcake pan, and then trying to resist the urge to eat them all directly out of the oven before frosting them. Try whipping up an Easter-themed batch with pastel colors and jellybeans on top, or make some birthday cupcakes with lots and lots of sprinkles. To be a real hero, bring your creations into work or class the next day.

Let In Some Fresh Air

Hanging out at home feels great, but every now and then all that time inside can also give you a touch of cabin fever. Fortunately, simply cracking a window and breathing in some new oxygen can be all it takes to feel reinvigorated in your own home. So when you're feeling cooped up, open up those windows or sit on your porch for a bit to refresh your lungs *and* spirit. The fresh air will also clear your home of staleness or cooking odors that you might not have noticed before. To take your house's air quality to the next level, you can also invest in an air purifier if you're prone to seasonal allergies, or a dehumidifier if your bathroom or closet gets a little damp.

Call a Parent

Seriously, what are you waiting for? Dial up your mom or dad for a heartfelt one-on-one. Spend some time catching up on each other's lives and be sure to give your appreciation for all they've done for you over the years.

Try a New Smartphone Game

Your phone's constant connection to social media might leave you feeling a little drained, but that doesn't mean you can't put it on do-not-disturb mode and use it as a personal video game device for the afternoon. Download a game you've been wanting to try and retreat from the world for a little bit.

Create a Personal Website

Having your own Internet presence can do wonders for your career growth. If you don't already have your own dot-com, register a domain and start creating your online headquarters with an easy-to-use website builder like Squarespace or Medium. You can make it work-focused, personality-driven—or anything in between.

Give Yourself a Face Massage

With some basic acupressure, you can dissolve facial tension, relax your jaw, and make these often neglected muscles feel oh-so-zen. First, wash your face and hands so you don't bring any unwanted oil into your pores. Next, apply pressure upward on your forehead toward your scalp, along your jaw in gentle circular motions, and on the back of your scalp at your hairline. Make sure to rub your tight neck muscles for an extra dose of relief. If you want, you can also use a gentle serum or face oil during the massage to get your skin super soft. Repeat whenever you're feeling stressed. *Ahhhhhhh.*

Have an "Ode to Chocolate" Night

You can throw a chocolate-themed party for friends, but no one will blame you for not wanting to share this one. For the main course, make chicken mole, which uses Mexican chocolate to add a savory hint of smoke to the dish. Serve with chocolate smoothies or milkshakes. For dessert, get creative! Make a smorgasbord of fudgy desserts, or whip up a big batch of cocoa and set up a toppings bar. Marshmallows are a must, but also consider caramel sauce, chocolate syrup, whipped cream, sprinkles, and candy canes for stirring.

Watch an Inspirational TED Talk

A whole library of motivational and thought-provoking messages are just moments away, thanks to your smartphone. Via TED, experts on everything from body language to quantum physics give influential lectures that can be as short as one minute, and as long as sixty. Choose your topic and change your world.

Have Breakfast in Bed...for Dinner

When it comes to eating, rules about when to have what are purely arbitrary. Pancakes, waffles, bacon, and scrambled eggs aren't just for before noon! Indulge in a morning feast at night, because life is too short to limit maple syrup to the a.m.

Practice Cartwheels

If you haven't tried doing this basic gymnastic move since you were young, give it another go (safely!) for fun. Even if you're not as flexible as you once were, you can still enjoy the challenge of a perfect cartwheel or handstand.

Host a Weekly Watch Party

TV series are perfect for binge watching, but remember how exciting it was to anticipate the next episode of your favorite show every Tuesday or Friday night, and watch it at the same time as the rest of the world? Enjoy the community aspect of group-watching a great show—without having to leave your couch—by having your friends come to you for a recurring date night with your TV. Invite a group over, serve themed snacks, dish about the plot during commercial breaks, and relish in how fun it is to actually watch a show live.

Learn a New Skill Via *YouTube*

Whether you want to learn how to build a computer, defend yourself, change a flat tire, or just take better photos for social media, there's a free video tutorial for that! Unlike a traditional hobby class or workshop, *YouTube* lets you pause, restart, and follow along at your own pace so you can really master your technique. You can use *YouTube* not only to teach yourself things you've always wanted to learn, but also to find new hobbies and skills you were completely unaware of. Glass blowing? Whistling with a blade of grass? Slam poetry? Your digital teachers are waiting!

Experiment with an Unusual Meditation

When most people picture meditation, sitting in the lotus position on your bedroom floor and chanting "om" comes to mind. But there are tons of ways to meditate that don't involve sitting or chanting! Try one of these creative techniques and feel its transformative effects:

- **Clean with intention.** Doing chores can be a meditative practice! As you sweep crumbs off the floor or wash dishes, focus on making slow, purposeful strokes with the broom or sponge. Try to put external thoughts out of your mind and channel all your worry into cleaning the object in front of you.
- **Walk with meaning.** Whether you're going down a busy city street or along a forest path, the meditative powers of walking can be restorative. Focus on the weight placed on your feet and the motion in your body as you transfer from left foot to right foot. Breathe deeply, roll your shoulders back, and let your mind center on the repetition of putting one foot in front of the other.
- **Shave with purpose.** Yes, shave! Your regular razor routine can be a surprising exercise in quiet and reflection. When you shave, you have to focus on only the act in front of you, not your thoughts. The next time you reach for your razor, use your strokes to concentrate on the mechanical act of moving it, putting your mind on pause.

Clip Coupons

You can save a ton of cash on everyday products! Stop tossing those grocery store fliers and start clipping. You can also check out one of the many couponing sites that have tons of tips for couponing newbies.

Watch *The Blind Side*

Make sure you have some tissues ready for this feel-good film. Sandra Bullock stars as a woman who takes in a homeless teen with a natural talent for football. Spend a couple hours being inspired by this touching true story.

Order Dinner In

While cooking can be a fun way to spend an evening, you can't play Julia Child *all* the time. Take a night off by having your favorite cuisine delivered hot right to your door—and never have to change out of your sweatpants.

Relax with a Homemade Face Mask

Bring the spa to you with an easy DIY face mask. Unlike more complicated spa regimens, this one only requires you to mix up a few items and apply the concoction to your face. You'll want to find a specific recipe online, but most include ingredients you likely already have on hand, like strawberries, egg whites, honey, avocado, raw sugar, and olive oil. In just a few steps, you'll have a pamper-ready, ultra-cheap mask for glowing, relaxed skin.

Handwrite Notes to Friends

Everyone loves getting snail mail! Letter writing is rarer than it used to be, sure, but that doesn't mean the joy of getting an unexpected personal note has diminished in the slightest. Write a short, just-to-say-hi letter, or a longer message, to mail the next time you are out. It will definitely brighten your friend or relative's day when they check their mailbox, fully expecting nothing but some more junk mail and credit card bills, and find your handwritten note. To keep up the habit, keep some greeting cards or stationery on hand so you'll be ready to mail out a personal letter whenever you get the urge.

Get a Little Crazy with Your Hairstyle

You'd never leave the house with a wild topknot or pigtails, you say? That's the point! Pick a day when you're not going out, sculpt a faux-hawk or make some silly curls, and chill out with your new 'do.

Read Dr. Seuss Books

There's a reason *Oh, the Places You'll Go!* is a popular graduation gift: Theodor Geisel's (a.k.a. Dr. Seuss) books offer valuable lessons for both actual kids *and* your own inner kid. Take some time to revisit the Seuss library and relish what you find that's relevant to your life now. "Today is your day!"

Sip Hot Water with Lemon

Research shows that this drink can help flush your system of toxins, reduce weight, and improve your complexion. But those benefits aside, it's also just a great way to hydrate, and is ultracomforting to sip. Add a touch of honey if you want a little sweetness.

Hang Twinkle Lights in Your Bedroom

It doesn't have to be a holiday to enjoy a little festive sparkle! Make your sleeping quarters a little dreamier by stringing up some twinkly lights in a soft yellow or fun rainbow colors. You can tack them onto a wall in a silhouette, border your window(s) and door, or create a headboard outline for your bed. You can also hang them above the bed like a canopy, or clip photos to each strand to make an ethereal photo display. You'll feel a little otherworldly delight every time you get back home after a long, hard day.

Draw a Cartoon

Even if stick figures are the upper limit of your drawing skills, bust them out and create a funny or pensive comic. Good cartooning is more about capturing the essence of your character or object than getting their entire likeness exactly right. Try your hand at drawing people, pets, and different objects. To send a message, you can turn your drawing into an editorial cartoon, or make it funny by creating a full comic strip. Remember, no one has to see this if you don't want them to (unless you discover your latent artistic calling and write the next *Garfield*!).

Have a Yard Sale

Make some extra money *and* clean out your unwanted stuff by selling it right out of your own house. First, gather up all of your gently used items, from kitchenware and clothing to old books and toys. Pick a day when the weather will be nice and advertise your sale through posters, online ads, or even just word of mouth. On the morning of, put out some lemonade or water and invite the neighbors to come discover a new treasure. You'll meet new people and clear out some room in your house without having to go farther than your garage.

Set Up a Blind Wine Tasting

Can your friends tell the difference between sauvignon blanc and pinot grigio? What if they're *blindfolded*? Score bottles of your favorite wines, and invite your friends over for some snacks and a fun guessing game that just happens to involve a delicious beverage. Wine not your thing? You can also do a taste test with different types of beer. To make the tasting blind, disguise each bottle in a paper bag or tightly wrapped aluminum foil and give it a numbered tag. (Make sure you've written down which is which on a master list!) Blindfold the contestants, pour each of them a small glass, and see who can correctly guess the type. Give winners the rest of the bottle to take home at the end of the night!

Embrace Loneliness

It sounds like a scam, right? How could anyone possibly *enjoy* the sensation of being all alone? Bear with me here, because if you can sit quietly with your feeling of being lonely—instead of fighting back against it or looking for a quick fix via your phone—you might discover a newfound inner peace. Follow these steps to embrace loneliness:

1 **Understand the truth about loneliness.** First, realize that the stigma that it's bad to be lonely is just that: a stigma. Everyone feels lonely from time to time, even busy parents or people whose lives always look bustling on social media.

2 **Look at the positives.** Embracing loneliness means being optimistic about the physical and mental space that being alone creates. You have time to get in touch with your thoughts, reflect on your goals, and even just dance around the house with no one there to give you the side eye. Strive to enjoy the peace—the feeling of boredom means that there's nothing going wrong.

3 **Let go.** Finally, try to release a little of your own introspection around feeling lonely. Sometimes the more you obsess over your own lack of companionship, the worse it seems. You deserve love and friendship and everything the world has to offer, and you have plenty of chances in the future to get out there and enjoy time with other people. So take a deep breath, and focus on the current opportunity to care for your own needs.

Play a Silly Instrument

Anyone can be a musical maestro on the kazoo, triangle, or recorder. Pick the goofy instrument of your choice and see if you can teach yourself a few songs. Even if you never make it to the *Billboard* charts, you'll have a lot of fun trying.

Have a Solo Eighties, or Nineties, or Aughts Night

Bask in nostalgia with a retro night in by yourself. Pick your favorite decade and decide whether you want a high-energy single dance party, delicious dinner party for one, or chill movie marathon that focuses on that time period. Make sure to dress for the occasion.

Learn How to Tie a Necktie

If you've never tied a necktie (or bow tie), it's a fun and useful skill to learn! With online diagrams, you'll be an expert at this swanky accessory in no time.

Read Missed Connections on *Craigslist*

You've probably browsed *Craigslist* for apartment rentals or used cars, but did you know it has personals too? Each day, thousands of people post a personal ad in the Missed Connections section, looking for an attractive stranger they recently spotted. Ads can range from funny ("Girl who dropped her ice cream on my foot at Baskin-Robbins") to a little heartbreaking ("I talked to you for hours at a concert but forgot to get your number"). It's hard not to secretly hope you recognize yourself in one of these stranger-to-stranger ads, but they make for great entertainment regardless!

Give Your Toes a Relaxing Soak

If you've never tried it, you might be surprised by how good a simple bucket of hot water can feel to your feet after a long day. A traditional foot soak uses a combo of hot water and Epsom salts, a dissolvable compound of magnesium and sulfate that removes toxins and soothes aches and pains. To give it a try, add ½ cup Epsom salts to a small basin or bucket of warm or hot (but not scalding) water, then start soaking your feet. For a real spa feel, add some drops of an essential oil to the bath and reap the benefits of calming aromatherapy.

Play a Practical Joke

The chance to pull off a lighthearted prank on your partner or good friend shouldn't go to waste! Below are some ideas for a little April Fool's–inspired humor (with varying levels of corniness). Just beware: Perpetrators may soon become the perpetrated...

- Put Bubble Wrap under a rug.
- Tell them you made brownies, and when they rush to the kitchen, uncover your pan of *E*'s cut out of brown cardboard or construction paper. Brown-*E*'s...get it?
- Fill doughnuts with mayonnaise instead of traditional filling.
- Install a browser extension on their laptop that turns every photo into a picture of Nicolas Cage. (This is a real thing.)
- Use instant mac and cheese powder and water to make a fresh glass of "orange juice" for them.
- Coat their bar of soap with a layer of clear nail polish so it won't lather.
- Sign them up for a funny mailing list.
- Put the TV remote or their favorite coffee mug in Jell-O.
- If they leave their soda or water bottle unattended, unscrew the cap, put plastic wrap over the lid, and replace the cap.

Watch the Sun Rise and Set

Bookend your day with a meditative reflection by watching the sun both rise that morning and set that night—pausing to ponder the beauty of the universe.

Read Hilarious *Amazon* Reviews

Stand-up comedy shows require money and, well, leaving your cozy home, but laughing at funny comments online is totally free. You can find tons of them hiding in the reviews section of shopping sites. Hint: Start by searching "banana slicer" on *Amazon*.

Give Your Dog a Bath

You love to pamper yourself, but isn't it about time Fido got a spa day too? If you don't have a dog yourself, offer to give a friend or family member's dog a good scrub-down.

Read *1Q84* by Haruki Murakami

Got a lot of couch time in your future? Good, because you'll want it to tackle this magnum opus by one of Japan's greatest writers. Your time will be well spent, of course, because Murakami's work is extraordinary. It follows Aomame, a woman who climbs down a highway exit and into an alternate reality where she's a swift-footed assassin. Her story intertwines with that of a writer named Tengo, who has a mysterious encounter with a younger girl who enters a fiction contest he is judging. Together, Aomame and Tengo make their way through a new strange world. You won't be able to put it down!

Create a Signature Drink

Quenching your thirst at home can be as easy as popping open a beer or seltzer, but every now and then it feels nice to treat yourself to something a little fancier. For those times, you'll want a go-to signature drink. Experiment with different liquors, juices, syrups, garnishes, and flavors to create a beverage that's all you. For a boozy libation, start with a base liquor like gin or whiskey, and then add whatever fresh juice or mixer you prefer, and a finish like bitters, herbs, or an edible garnish. For a mocktail version, you can test different juices, tonics, and sodas until you land on a tasty combination you'll want to pour again and again.

Challenge Friends to a Word Game Night

Scrabble, Boggle, Upwords, Words with Friends: Pick your poison and challenge your favorite wordsmiths to a few rounds of friendly competition.

Make Someone Laugh

Prove that laughter really is the best medicine by texting a friend a funny photo, calling a family member and reminiscing over a hilarious memory, or bonding over an inside joke with your partner. A great belly laugh is one of the sincerest gifts you can give!

Plan Your Own World Record

There's a bar set for every weird talent you can think of, from the longest handshake to the tallest mohawk. Look up the funniest, freakiest, and most impressive world records and choose your favorites. Which ones could you break? Bonus points if you actually attempt a new record!

Find a Part-Time Job to Do at Home

The downside of most jobs is that you have to actually get dressed and go places. Thankfully, if you're looking for a side hustle to make extra money and/or fill free time, there's tons of part-time work you can do right from your couch. Take a look at these ideas to get started:

- **Transcribing audio.** Several online services let users upload their audio files and get a transcription of the file's text emailed back to them. That transcriptionist could be you! The work usually pays decently and can often be done on your own timeline.
- **Pet sitting.** Through services like Rover.com, you can sign up to watch adorable pets while their owners are traveling. Having a cute dog or cat in your space will provide you with some cuddly companionship, and pet owners can rest easy knowing their fur babies are in fantastic hands.
- **Website testing.** UserTesting.com is just one site that companies use for paid focus group testing of their websites or apps. It's all done remotely, so you can perform and record your testing at noon or midnight, from your couch or hammock.
- **Online teaching.** If you're an expert in a particular subject matter, you can sign up to teach college courses online. You won't have to get up in front of a classroom; instead, you'll grade papers remotely and even give lectures over video chat.

Make a Batch of Cold Brew Coffee

Stop spending mega bucks and time at coffee shops by DIYing your own cold brew coffee. Cold brew is less acidic than normal coffee, making it a perfectly smooth and refreshing pick-me-up. And it couldn't be simpler to make in your own kitchen! In a big jar or bowl, combine water and coarsely ground coffee beans. (Try ½ pound coffee beans and ½ gallon cold water to start.) Let the mixture steep overnight in the refrigerator, then strain it in the morning into a clean container. You're done! Reward your labor with a big cup, then continue to enjoy your homemade caffeine fix whenever you feel the urge.

Play Charades

Sometimes the best games involve good friends, zero screens, and zero equipment. Enter charades! All you need for this seriously entertaining game is three or more other people. To play, divide into two or more teams and take turns acting out different people, movies, shows, places, and more for your teammates to guess. Set a phone timer each round so teammates only have a certain number of seconds to guess correctly. You can also write charade scenarios on scraps of paper beforehand so everyone just has to draw from the deck at the start of their turn.

Host a Video Game Tournament

You can battle your partner, or invite some friends over for a team contest. Whether your game is *Mario Kart* or *Call of Duty*, suit up for some competition full of laughs—and some playful trash-talking.

Throw an Indoor Picnic

Eat a tasty spread inside where the ants won't find it! Spread a blanket on the floor, pack a basket of snacks, and have a fun ground-level feast sans bugs and sunburns.

Pop Bubble Wrap

It was so satisfying when you were a kid, and it will still be satisfying now!

Color Your Worries Away

Remember when your biggest worry was what color to make the flowers in a garden scene you were coloring? Adult coloring books are fun, but sometimes you just need a night with crayons and Winnie-the-Pooh to take the edge off of adulthood. In fact, the hobby you loved as a kid can be just as rewarding and even soothing now; studies show that coloring can reduce anxiety and even lower depression symptoms. So grab some colored pencils or crayons and color your way to calm.

Watch *Good Will Hunting*

It's always fun to revisit the earlier works of actors who have become household names. Matt Damon and Ben Affleck hit it big with their first screenplay in 1997's *Good Will Hunting*, a drama about a young and troubled Boston man with genius-level math skills. The film was nominated for nine Academy Awards the year of its release, and opened to universal favorable reviews. If you haven't seen Robin Williams's turn as an eccentric but patient therapist, or Damon and Affleck's excellent Boston accents, fire this one up pronto. And even if you have, it's always worth the rewatch.

Listen to a Motown Hit

The Motown label was formed by Berry Gordy Jr. in 1959, and its music has become synonymous with not only some of the best records of all time, but also African-American culture in Detroit, Michigan. The Supremes, the Jackson 5, Marvin Gaye, Stevie Wonder, Aretha Franklin, Diana Ross: Some of America's greatest artists rose to fame under this label. And besides making catchy songs, Motown's smash success played a pivotal role in racial integration in the pop music community. Revisit some of your favorite classic singles and sing along—no one's there to judge!

Make Sustainable Changes Around Your Home

Just a few easy swaps can make your space a little nicer to the environment. Some ideas:

- Swap incandescent light bulbs for compact fluorescent light bulbs or LEDs. These newer, more sustainable versions last up to fifty times longer than traditional options.
- Reduce your water use by installing faucet aerators and low-flow showerheads.
- Make sure your windows are well sealed in the winter to prevent losing energy through drafts. You'll also save on your utility bill!
- Buy a programmable thermostat to keep the air-conditioning or heat lower when you're not at home.

Start a Pillow Fight

Just because you haven't had a pillow fight in years doesn't mean now's not a good time to rediscover the magic of this childhood favorite. Grab a friend and a pillow and start swinging!

Memorize US Presidents

You might have learned a catchy mnemonic song in grade school to remember the order of these commanders in chief, but see if you can recall all of them now. If not, head over to *YouTube* to learn a new version of the song.

Bake Gooey Chocolate Chip Cookies

There are few problems that can't be solved with a big, warm, tasty chocolate chip cookie right out of the oven. What are you waiting for?!

Make Jewelry

Skip the overpriced jewelry in stores *and* delve into a new craft by teaching yourself the art of jewelry-making. Beads and wire, or leather and metal accents, plus a few easy-to-find tools are all you need to start crafting your own sparkly, sophisticated, or sleek accessories. Try your hand at making some simple pendant necklaces, earrings, bracelets, watchbands, or cuff links in whatever style you choose. Even if you're not a big jewelry wearer yourself, you can give your creations away as gifts to friends or a partner, or even set up your own jewelry store at a craft fair or online marketplace like *Etsy*.

Learn a Card Trick

Impress everyone at your next party by whipping out a little sleight of hand. With a deck of cards and a bit of practice, you can master some of the basic tricks that you may have seen on TV. Card tricks are a great icebreaker for any crowd, and you'll get a huge self-confidence boost from seeing your audience's stunned, impressed faces. There are tons of free online tutorials you can use to get your David Copperfield on. Who knows, you may even work your way up to being a magician in a side hustle. Remember: Never give away your secrets!

Read Old Messages from a Loved One

Think of previous conversations on your phone or computer as mini time capsules. Whether they're old AOL messages, texts, or good ol' love letters written on paper, revisit fond memories by going through your relationship archives.

Listen to a Classical Composer

Whether it's Mozart, Bach, or Brahms, relax with the soothing sounds of a symphony by one of the greats. If you're a newbie to classical music, search your music streaming service for "classical music 101" or find a curated playlist to get you started.

Perfect Your Shower Vocals

When you're alone in your bathroom, no one can hear you over-shoot a B-flat. Use your cleansing time to practice those harmonies and get your pitch-perfect rendition of "My Heart Will Go On" down for your imaginary audience of millions.

Suds It Up with Homemade Soap

A bar of Irish Spring or Dove isn't nearly as fun to lather up with as soap that you've crafted and customized yourself. Homemade soap isn't as complicated as it may sound, either: It's essentially a combination of lye with an oil or a fat that is then left to harden. The most popular way to make your own is the cold-process method.

Before starting, you'll need proper safety equipment—lye can be dangerous, so it's important to wear goggles and gloves while working.

Specific steps will vary depending on the recipe, but most will have you combine the lye and water, then add in your chosen fats or oils and any extras. You will then pour the mixture into a mold to set for twenty-four to thirty-six hours. After, the soap will need to cure in open air for about four weeks. Once it's done, you can slice it up and get to washing! You can find tons of great cold-process recipes online that use everything from dried citrus and herbs to goat's milk and tea to make soaps you'll be obsessed with.

Feeling too impatient to make bar soap? Liquid shower gel can be made in just a few minutes using castile soap and essential oils. You'll get your custom soap without any of the waiting around.

Write a Haiku

Remember the five-seven-five poem you wrote in grade school? (That's five syllables on the first line, seven syllables on the second line, and five syllables on the third.) Get back into the art of this simple poem style by trying your hand at a few haikus. They don't have to rhyme!

Post a Life Affirmation

From literary quotes to mantras from *RuPaul's Drag Race*, everyone has a saying that makes them feel ready to conquer the world. Write one down on a sticky note and post it where you will see it every day. Time to reach for the stars!

Eat Something Green

Have you heard of the benefits of leafy greens? Kale, spinach, chard, and collard greens all pack a hefty punch of iron, calcium, and vitamin A, so eat up. Okay, fine: Green Sour Patch Kids count too.

Listen to Episodes of *Heavyweight*

If you're on the hunt for a new (or first) podcast but are unsure what topics will interest you, *Heavyweight* is a great place to start. Jonathan Goldstein narrates this gripping podcast about helping two people in conflict bury the hatchet in all kinds of creative ways. Each episode will keep you coming back for more raw emotion, touching stories, and unexpected humor. Pro tip: Cue up the "Gregor" episode first. It follows Goldstein and his friend Gregor as they try to get CDs back that Gregor once lent to music artist Moby.

Have a Nerf Battle

There's nothing like an adrenaline rush to bring you closer to someone you love. So grab the foam weapon of your choice, because it's *on*. Feel free to create your own set of rules before your battle, like no aiming at faces or no physical contact. You can also upgrade your battle concept with a theme like zombies vs. humans! Use cardboard boxes or tables as bunkers, and be sure to move any breakable objects out of the way. Engage your partner in some lighthearted combat around your house until someone surrenders. The loser has to make dinner!

Watch Clouds Float By

You don't need other people around to contemplate the role you play in the big picture. Take a few minutes to lie or sit on some fresh grass and watch the sky for a spiritual moment of reflection.

Learn How to Juggle

It's harder than it looks! But with this time inside and some solid online tutorials, you will keep all of your (literal) balls in the air with the best of them.

Host a Monopoly Tournament

If you've played Monopoly, you know that you'll want to allot a good amount of time for this one. Make sure you have plenty of snacks on hand and invite some friends over for a classic battle over real estate. If you get tired, you can always take a break and come back for more later.

Throw a Surprise Party

Give one of your besties a super sweet surprise they'll never for-get! By hosting it at your place, you can control the planning, the details, and the surprise itself, so everything can go off without a hitch. Whether it's a birthday, going-away party, or celebration for a job promotion, here are the elements you will need to focus on:

- **Planning.** You'll need to pick the date and time, and send out invites. Most importantly, make sure no one accidentally clues your friend in to what's happening! Be careful to omit your guest of honor from the invites list.
- **The big surprise.** Have the guest of honor "stop by" your place to pick you up for dinner, or invite them over for "dessert." Ensure the other partygoers arrive at least thirty minutes in advance and are hidden before the big arrival. *Surprise!*
- **Party time.** Keep your actual party simple and fun with some finger foods, cupcakes, and upbeat music so the focus can stay on the guest of honor! You can shop for the decor, food, and drinks yourself, or designate people to bring different items.

Answer Questions Online

Use your professional or personal expertise to help others find the thoughtful answers they're looking for on sites like *Yahoo! Answers* and *Quora*. You never know what experiences you might have that could benefit someone else!

Sing Along to a Musical

It doesn't matter if you can't hit all the notes that Julie Andrews does in *The Sound of Music*; singing in your own home is all about fun, not perfection. Belt out your favorite show tunes and picture yourself taking a bow on Broadway after your solo.

Up Your Grilled Cheese Game

All you need is a skillet, bread, and cheese to get your cozy on at home. But you can also give your sandwich a little something special by adding a fancier cheese or different extras like tomato and pesto, avocado and bacon, or ham and grilled pineapple.

Bring the Drive-In to You

You know what's even better than watching a movie on your couch? Watching one on a mega screen outside on a warm night. To make your own personal big-screen theater, rent or borrow a movie projector—sometimes you can even check one out at your local public library—and play your favorite film on the side of your house, a bedsheet hung up on a wall, or your garage door. (Plug in some headphones if it's too hard to hear or you don't want to disturb your neighbors.) Snuggle into a sleeping bag or recline in a lawn chair and have an extra-special movie night. Don't forget the popcorn!

Read the News

Even though the news can be a roller coaster of emotions, staying informed is an important part of feeling connected to the world around you. Take some time to get up to speed on today's current events. Even if politics aren't your cup of tea, there's way more going on out there than legislation. If you're not a traditional print newspaper person, you can get your news online with an app like Apple News, or support good journalism through an online subscription to a legacy publication like *The New York Times* or *The Washington Post*.

Set Up a Game of Ping-Pong

With two paddles and a net, you can turn any table into a Ping-Pong battlefield. It might not be regulation size (that would be five feet by nine feet), but you don't need an official setup to have a ton of fun with a friend or partner.

Design a Costume for Your Pet

Can you turn a bulldog into a bumblebee? Or a cat into a Christmas elf? Whether you use your brainstorming to order a costume online or DIY it, there will definitely be pics that are too cute *not* to post on social media.

Cook a Meal for Your Family

Pay your family back in kindness—and good food—by inviting them over for a casual meal to thank them for all they've done for you over the years. Make a big, crowd-pleasing pot of chili or paella and spend your time reminiscing about good days past.

Do a Smartphone JOMO Makeover

Trying to cut back on your screen time when you always have a smartphone nearby is a struggle. Luckily, there are some great tips out there to help you check in on your phone a little less, and remain in the present moment a little more! Check them out:

- Change your call and text ringtones for the people closest to you. Ignore the others until you're ready to touch base.
- When you're in an elevator or waiting in line, take a mini meditation moment with your thoughts or chat with someone nearby instead of pulling out your phone.
- Delete any apps you haven't used in ages and organize existing ones into folders that you have to click through every time you want to use an app (especially social media ones!).
- Make your home screen as minimal as possible. Consider keeping all of your apps and folders on a second page so you don't even see them when you open your phone.
- Turn off push notifications. It'll force you to manually refresh your apps when you want to see new photos or emails. (You can keep a few important ones on if necessary, like calls from your spouse.)
- Put your phone in a different room while you read or watch TV. Curling up with a book when your phone is only inches away is a recipe for getting lost in *Instagram*. Keep your device out of sight, out of mind so you can focus on the book or show in front of you.
- Use a real alarm clock instead of the alarm on your smartphone. Then, charge your phone overnight either across the room or in a different room so you won't be tempted to scroll through social media before bed or as soon as you wake up.

Build a Replica of Your Home

It's harder than you think! Try using LEGOs, clay, or blocks to re-create your apartment, house, or even your childhood home.

Eat All Three Meals Outside

Breakfast on your front porch, lunch on the back patio, and picnic dinner in your backyard, maybe? Try having your meals under the open sky for some quality time with nature while still eating pasta.

Take Deep Breaths

Breathe in slowly through your nose. Breathe out slowly through your mouth. Repeat. Soak up the present moment as you breathe, and say a word of gratitude for where you are right now, right this second. The outside world can wait until you're ready to face it again.

Index

About the Author

A native of Ohio and Florida, Jessica Misener is a senior editor whose writing has appeared on *BuzzFeed*, *HuffPost*, *Cosmopolitan*, *The Atlantic*, and more. She's also worked as a T-shirt folder, dry cleaning assistant, grocery store cashier, librarian, and ancient Greek tutor. She lives in Brooklyn, New York, where she regularly eats twice her weight in burritos.